Mastering Embodied Flow Mindset: Unleashing Peak Performance Potential in Sports and Life

How Extreme Sports Athletes Foster Flow for Success in Athletics, Business, and Daily Life

Johnna Haskell

Published by: Epic Leaf Innovations LLC

To request permissions, contact the publisher at epicleafinnovations.com

Hardcover: 978-1-964562-01-8

Paperback: 978-1-964562-00-1

Table of Contents

Introduction

Do you ever find yourself so deeply immersed in an activity that time seems to stand still? Have you experienced moments where your skills and the challenge at hand merge seamlessly, and the world around you fades away? Are you haunted by fleeting glimpses of your true potential, leaving you hungry for more?

Do you sense a whispered yearning deep within your soul, calling you toward something far more profound and electrifying than the mundane, stress-filled existence that so many settle for? Have you tasted the exhilaration of being fully alive and present, only to wonder how to make those precious moments of flow a consistent part of your life?

Perhaps you keep these aspirations hidden, fearing others would consider you crazy or delusional for daring to believe you were made for something far greater. Yet still, the unshakable sense remains, an inextinguishable knowing that an exhilarating reality beyond your current limitations is not only possible—but also your embodied potential. This potential, rooted in your natural affinities and passions, propels you toward pursuing and mastering your unique talents.

This primordial longing is calling you toward the rarified realm of "embodied flow"—a harmonic merging of mind and body, where your capabilities operate at their highest heights—where you become utterly absorbed in the present-moment sublime of the creative process itself. In those moments of flow consciousness, you lose your rigid identity in the ecstatic joy of bringing a unique vision into masterful material form. Challenge and skill unite as you enter pure presencing and flow.

Yet for most, this coveted territory of embodied flow remains extremely elusive. Despite brief glimpses that only intensify the fires of yearning further, the ability to consciously access and sustain these peak states of absorption and performance appears nearly impossible to achieve—an enormous, seemingly fruitless struggle.

As someone who has dedicated their life to exploring the farthest frontiers of human potential, I have witnessed firsthand the mind-boggling feats made possible through the unwavering pursuit of embodied flow. From elite athletes like rock climbers Alex Honnold and Tommy Caldwell scaling the blankest, sheerest rock faces without ropes in a seamless dance of real-time risk calculation and technical mastery... to authors like Maya Angelou placing their tormented souls on raw display through the transcendent medium of poetic language and metaphor... to musicians like John Coltrane and Jimi Hendrix riding a spontaneous wave of improvisation into realms of sonic expression that have yet to be replicated...

Those luminaries featured in this book have shattered our conventional frameworks around the limits of human performance, creativity, and consciousness expansion. They have expanded the territory of what is possible by harnessing the power of embodied flow.

Still, their accomplishments are not merely results of elite-level skills, talents, or even fearlessness. Rather, they stem from a profound embodied expertise—an instinctive integration of conscious presencing and flow that allows them to merge seamlessly with their chosen medium. It is an ability to attune with fluid responsiveness to the ever-shifting complexities and micro-demands of their crafts—a preternatural trust and harmonization with the intuitive intelligence of the lived experience itself.

And you too can unearth this rarified experience of being. This book is your guide to embarking on the same transformative journey toward embodied-flow immersion that these luminaries have walked.

Within these pages lies a comprehensive roadmap to unearth your own embodied flow awakening. Drawing from my multifaceted odyssey as an adventurer, researcher, and educator—fortified by decades of research and hard-won wisdom—you'll explore the enactive approach. This way of being brings the perceptual mind–body experience and the body's dynamic engagement with the environment into purposeful, reciprocal interaction to cultivate embodied flow.

You'll also gain rare insights into how elite athletes and other luminaries across extreme pursuits like adventure sports, improvised music, dance, and the creative arts have refined their ability to access flow. From there, you can discover possible pathways to forge your own cultivation by applying their principles to catalyze creativity, emotional mastery, leadership excellence, and overall flourishing across any life domain. The transformative power of embodied flow is by no means limited to those upper echelons alone.

As artist Robert Henri (1923) expressed, "The object isn't to make art, it's to be in that wonderful state which makes art inevitable." This quest into embodied mastery ultimately represents a profound awakening—one that reunites us with the full spectrum of our latent capacities.

When you embrace flow as a holistic experience emerging from the integration of a focused mind, an attuned body, and an ineffable openness to the present mystery, you open the doorway to profound personal awakening. You reunite with the full spectral range of your latent human capacities and potential for flourishing at the highest levels.

In our modern age that so often disconnects us from our deepest callings and innate wisdom, cultivating flow consciousness provides a journey back to your essential truth and wholeness. It is a way to rediscover the core of who you are—a homecoming for your fully integrated being.

In those priceless moments of achieving flow, you catch breathtaking glimpses of the infinite creative possibilities still dormant within you— fields of potential yearning to blossom into manifest expression. You become a living, breathing reminder of an ancient truth—that your boundless human capacities emerge not from chasing some imagined future state, but from your wholehearted, embodied commitment to the journey of the present unfolding here and now.

My initiations into the exhilarating depths of flow began at an early age amid the vast, untamed landscapes of nature. As an obsessive ice climber, mountaineer, skier, and aviator constantly hungry for transcendent experience, I found myself repeatedly brushing up against this altered state that permanently reshaped my apertures of perception.

On the towering alpine faces, flow arrived as a delicate dance between life and death—those rare glimpses where I could quiet all the voices as every movement became fluid, intuitive poetry inscribed into the vertical stone. In the roiling turbulence of the atmosphere, while flying, flow unveiled itself as the unwavering stillness of a pilot utterly synchronizing with the rhythms of wind, clouds, and gravity in complete attunement.

One of my most intense wake-up calls to the razor-thin line separating challenge from breakthrough occurred during an attempted climb of the infamous Ushba peak in Russia with legendary mountaineer Scott Fischer. Trapped in a fierce storm just below the summit, we decided that descending the next morning would be safest—while the glacier remained stable before warming temperatures brought instability.

As our team traversed an exposed, crevasse-riddled section obscured by swirling snow, disaster struck without warning. The entire snow bridge supporting Fischer's footsteps suddenly collapsed beneath him. I was the last climber maintaining tension on our rope line. In an instant, the failing bridge violently whiplashed me airborne before I could even process what happened—a terrifying plummet into the abyss.

With Fischer leading our line and one climber between us, the sheer force whipped that middle climber past Scott, while I found myself flung a staggering 150–200 ft farther down the slope. There we dangled over the void, those sickening split seconds where the edge between life and death gets decided.

But in that breathtaking moment suspended between catastrophe and survival, Fischer's lifetime of extreme climbing experience took over. With unification-level precision, he planted his ax at the last possible instant, miraculously stopping our deadly plummet mere inches from oblivion.

Hanging there defying the odds, adrenaline flooded me as disappointment crashed over not arresting the fall sooner. Yet Fischer remained poised, his iconic wry grin steadying us both. I recalled our earlier conversation when we didn't reach the summit: It wasn't about the height or altitude achieved, but the attitude brought to the challenge. That profound calm readiness embodied in this moment.

The unknown lies under every step out here, I recalled him saying evenly. It's how we embrace uncertainty. Keep pushing the limits of what we're capable of achieving. His perspective landed with a jolt of recognition.

This was the required mindset: not shrinking from risks, but leaning into the unknown as a normal state of being, continually expanding skills and experience to match the greatest challenges I could envision, and asking myself, *What are my true limits? What heights of mastery might I achieve if I wholeheartedly commit?* Only by cultivating that unwavering preparedness to meet uncertainty head-on could I hope to thrive on the razor's edge separating disaster from breakthrough.

That precarious sweet spot is where embodied flow lives—a rarified frequency where our greatest challenges and deepest capacities unite in perfect synchrony. We operate in a transcendent realm of being, riding the leading edge of the present moment with complete, spontaneous presence. It's here that we tap the hidden wellsprings of genius innately pulsing within, just waiting to be unleashed.

The path of embodied-flow development is not for the timid, lukewarm, or uncommitted. It will test you to the very depths of your soul, demanding that you relinquish all delusions of control and cherished identities rooted in limiting beliefs and avoidance patterns. You will be forced to fearlessly confront the deepest wells of fear, anger, grief, and insecurity that lie dormant within your psyche—to shatter the mental and somatic shackles that keep you imprisoned in imposed limitations.

The journey has arrived at a critical crossroads, with a singularly defining choice now before you: Will you merely breathe the surface wisps of your true power and potential? Settling for watered-down versions of your dreams and faltering before the fires of real transformation? Or will you turn and face the razor's edge that separates the evasion of your limited perceptions from the breathtaking truth of your ultimate human potential?

Commit fully to the ultimate adventure of awakening—allowing the transcendent power of flow to remake you from the deepest quantum levels of your consciousness until you embody radiant presence, creative genius, and unwavering resilience in any circumstance.

The decision rests with you. The limitless wellspring of human potential resides within, awaiting only the spark of your wholehearted consent to unleash it. All that remains is the whole being-ness of your soul's resounding "Yes!"

If that resonates, let's discover what the unique blueprint of your path to embodied flow will look like!

Chapter 1:

The Flow Blueprint

Throughout this chapter, we'll demystify the science and practice of flow, drawing upon the groundbreaking insights of Mihaly Csikszentmihalyi and other pioneers in the field. We'll explore the key principles and triggers that give rise to optimal experience, and discover how to apply them across diverse areas of life, from work and play to personal growth and relationships.

As we venture deeper into the heart of flow, we'll encounter inspiring stories of individuals who have harnessed its power to achieve the extraordinary—from athletes who push the boundaries of human performance to artists who create works of breathtaking beauty. Through their examples, we'll learn that flow isn't just a fleeting peak experience, but a way of life that can be cultivated and sustained.

Flow in the Zone

The flow experience represents a transient blurring of the boundaries between self and activity, a merging of consciousness and present-moment engagement. Mihaly Csikszentmihalyi (1990), the psychologist who popularized the concept, described it as "a sense of effortless action in the moment" characterized by intense focus, distortion of temporal experience, and a profound sense of control and fulfillment.

Embodied flow arises when we strike an optimal balance between the challenges before us and our developed skills to meet those challenges. It's a sweet spot where our abilities are stretched but not overwhelmed, allowing us to surrender into an intuitive groove of heightened functioning. In this state, our bodily movements and sensations are seamlessly integrated with our mental processes, creating a sense of unity between mind, body, and the task at hand (Colombetti, 2014).

Neurologically speaking, embodied flow involves a dynamic reorchestration of brain networks. The default mode network (DMN), associated with referential thought and mind-wandering, temporarily quiets down, while the task-positive network (TPN), governing outward attention and sensorimotor integration, lights up in a coordinated symphony of highly focused engagement (Wotruba et al., 2014). This neural shift facilitates the heightened proprioception, effortless movement, and full-body immersion characteristic of embodied flow. Csikszentmihalyi (1990) beautifully described this as "being so involved in an activity that nothing else seems to matter." We will explore this phenomenon in greater depth in the following section.

In embodied flow, our proprioceptive awareness heightens, our movements become spontaneous and unconscious, and we taste the indescribable joy of being fully alive and immersed in the present rhythm of our experience. This heightened bodily awareness often manifests as changes in muscle tension, breathing patterns, and heart rate, reflecting the body's attunement to the demands of the moment.

World-class performers across disciplines speak of accessing an almost transcendent flow experience, where their bodily movements and instincts are perfectly aligned with the challenges they face. Elite athletes enter "the zone," where the game seems to slow down and their actions unfold with uncanny ease, their proprioception and kinesthetic sense guiding their every move. Virtuoso musicians transcend the divide between instrument and self, their fingers dancing across the keys or strings with effortless precision. Programmers code in a rapturous trance—their keystrokes flowing in perfect harmony with their mental algorithms.

Among these extraordinary individuals, I love how vividly big-wave surfing legend Laird Hamilton embodies the transcendent experience of flow. When paddling into one of the ocean's towering liquid giants, Hamilton describes entering a profound state of present-moment attunement to the primal energies uncoiling before him.

In those moments, the chatter of the conscious mind falls utterly silent, as he becomes exquisitely immersed in reading the ever-shifting geometry of peaks, troughs, and currents. His body moves with a spontaneous, supernatural grace, each micro-adjustment and impulse materializing fluidly in response to the changing conditions. Despite the life-or-death stakes of the slightest miscalculation, Hamilton experiences a paradoxical lucidity and sense of control. It's like his unconscious mind takes over. Years of training and repetition have coded the skills into his neurology and muscles. Just as we don't ponder how to ride a bike, his deeply coded skills require no conscious thought, allowing him to simply react and move fluidly with the energy of the wave.

Hamilton's ability to manage treacherous, dynamic environments with split-second precision while remaining calm and present exemplifies embodied flow in its most extreme form. The conscious mind's controlling tendencies are temporarily transcended, allowing his finely tuned instincts and spontaneous responsiveness to take the wheel.

On a pragmatic note, flow isn't solely the province of savants and prodigies. Each of us has likely glimpsed this experience, however fleetingly, while immersed in a riveting novel, settled into the meditative cadence of a workout routine, or utterly absorbed in creative play as children before consciousness cast its long shadow.

Having explored the embodied experience of flow, let us now delve into the specific characteristics and conditions that define flow according to Csikszentmihalyi's model.

Flow Defined

To illustrate the concept of flow, Csikszentmihalyi presents a diagram that maps the relationship between challenges and skills, two key variables that determine our emotional state during an activity. The model suggests that our emotional experience is largely determined by the balance, or lack thereof, between the perceived challenges of a task and our own skill level in that domain.

According to Csikszentmihalyi's (1990) mode, there are eight distinct emotional states that arise from different combinations of challenge and skill levels:

- **Apathy:** Low challenge, low skill—a sense of disengagement and lack of motivation. Individuals feel indifferent and unmotivated because the task neither interests them nor requires any significant effort.

- **Boredom**: Low challenge, medium skill—feeling at ease but not particularly stimulated as the task does not engage individuals' full capabilities.

- **Relaxation:** Low challenge, high skill—a state of relaxation. Individuals feel comfortable and at ease because they can handle the task effortlessly.

- **Worry:** Medium challenge, low skill—a sense of concern or unease. Individuals feel concerned or uneasy because they doubt their ability to meet the challenge.

- **Anxiety:** High challenge, low skill—overwhelming stress and anxiety. Individuals feel overwhelmed and stressed because the demands of the task far exceed their capabilities.

- **Arousal:** High challenge, medium skill—a heightened sense of excitement and engagement, which often serves as a precursor to entering embodied flow.

- **Flow:** High challenge, high skill—complete absorption, focus, and effortless performance.

- **Control:** Medium challenge, high skill—a sense of control. Individuals feel mastery and control over the activity, handling the task competently and confidently.

In particular, when challenges are low and our skills are underdeveloped, we may find ourselves in a state of apathy. For students, this could look like the superstar athlete coasting through an elementary gym class with glazed-over disengagement, the class feeling like a chore.

As our skills grow but the challenges remain low, we may transition into a state of relaxation, where we feel at ease but not particularly stimulated. A gifted math student may experience this boredom while brilliantly but robotically solving the same algebraic equations shown for the fifth time, waiting to be truly challenged. However, when challenges outpace our current skill level, we may experience worry or anxiety, perceiving the demands as exceeding our capabilities.

This can happen to a writer staring down a scholarly thesis after only scratching out basic essays. Or a science student confronted with advanced computational models far beyond what they've mastered. Such a divide between challenges and skills can lead to a sense of overwhelm and stress. Like an unprepared student in advanced sculptural design, paralyzed before the complexity of chiseling delicate marble forms after mere beginner training. Or a dancer pushed onto the stage for a brutally choreographed routine without sufficient preparation.

As our skills develop to meet the increasing challenges, we may move into a state of arousal—a heightened sense of excitement and engagement. This is often the precursor to flow, as we begin to stretch ourselves and push the boundaries of our abilities. The flow state emerges when both challenges and skills are high, creating a sweet spot where we are fully immersed in the activity, our attention is focused, and our performance feels effortless yet highly effective.

However, finding the right degree of skilled challenge is crucial. While a four percent increase over our current capabilities may open the flow channel during normal training, too big a stretch can shut us down (Kotler, 2022). Conversely, during periods of injury or recovery, a smaller one to two percent challenge level may be more appropriate to avoid overexertion while still maintaining an engaged presence.

In his earlier work, *Beyond Boredom and Anxiety*, Csikszentmihalyi delves deeper into the nature of flow and its relationship to motivation and engagement. He argues that flow experiences are intrinsically rewarding—we pursue them for the sake of the experience itself, rather than for external rewards or validation (Csikszentmihalyi, 1975). When we enter the flow experience, we lose our consciousness and become fully absorbed in the present moment. Time seems to distort, with hours passing like minutes or moments stretching out into eternity. We feel a sense of control and mastery over the activity, even as it challenges us to the edge of our abilities.

All in all, Csikszentmihalyi's flow model provides a valuable framework for understanding the relationship between challenges, skills, and emotional experiences. By recognizing the conditions that promote flow experiences—namely, a balance between high challenges and high skills—we can more deliberately structure our activities and environments to increase the likelihood of entering and sustaining this optimal consciousness.

However, the flow experience is not a single, uniform phenomenon. Instead, it is a multifaceted one with various interconnected dimensions.

To gain a deeper understanding of what it means to be in flow, we must explore the key qualities that characterize this state.

In the next section, we will explore the rich texture of the flow experience. As we deconstruct flow into its core components, we can develop a more nuanced and practical understanding of how to develop this optimal experience in our own lives.

Nine Qualities of Flow

While the phenomenon of flow may at first appear elusive and transcendent, psychologist Csikszentmihalyi's pioneering work revealed a set of distinct qualities that characterize this absorbed state of peak performance. Deconstructing flow into nine key dimensions provides a comprehensive framework for recognizing, understanding, and ultimately developing this rewarding experience across diverse domains.

Just as we start as clumsy beginners when learning any new skill, like a child first wobbling on a bicycle with training wheels, entering the flow experience follows a similar progression. The nine qualities we will explore represent milestones along the journey from awkward novice to unconscious mastery and immersion.

In the sections that follow, we will explore each of these nine qualities in depth, drawing insights from my personal journey of learning to Nordic ski. Through these anecdotes, I will illustrate how the abstract concepts of flow play out in the concrete challenges and breakthroughs of skill development. As we explore the nuances of each quality, I invite you to reflect on your own path, considering how these qualities have manifested in your most immersive and rewarding experiences.

1. Challenge–Skill Balance

Entering a flow experience requires finding an ideal balance between the task's challenge level and our personal skill level. Should a task prove too easy, we may lose interest or become bored. Conversely, if the challenge vastly outmatches our current abilities, anxiety, and frustration can disrupt our flow. The sweet spot arises when the activity's demands stretch our skills just enough to captivate our undivided attention while still feeling achievable.

In my own journey of learning to Nordic ski, I remember my first wobbly attempts sliding across the snow. The simple act of remaining upright and balanced while navigating minor bumps and inclines occupied my full attention and effort. My skills, limited to basic balance and coordination, were challenged plenty by the unfamiliar gliding motions and equipment. At this early stage, achieving any state of flow was out of reach, overshadowed by the very real threats of falling and colliding with other skiers.

However, as I invested time into practicing the fundamentals and developing muscle memory, my baseline skills gradually expanded. The sheer novelty and unpredictability that previously dominated my awareness gave way to an increasing sense of control. Hills and turns that had felt unmanageable just days before became opportunities to refine edging techniques and experiment with poles. In those moments of dynamic matching between progressing skills and stimulating challenges, I began to taste the first glimpses of flow—a sense of empowered focus free from the earlier performance anxiety.

2. Merging of Action and Awareness

In our everyday lives, it's common to experience a conscious split between our actions and our awareness of those actions. We may perform a task while simultaneously judging and analyzing our own performance from a detached perspective. In flow, however, this dualistic fragmentation of consciousness dissolves. Action and awareness merge into a unified field of engagement with the current instant.

This merging of action and awareness can be observed across various domains, from artistic creation to athletic performance. Consider a painter, wholly engrossed in the process of bringing a canvas to life. As the artist's brush dances across the surface, their awareness becomes one with the unfolding interplay of colors, textures, and forms. Similarly, a musician lost in the throes of improvisation experiences a thoughtful merging of action and awareness, with each note and chord progression arising effortlessly as a spontaneous expression of their inner world.

Within the sports arena, a figure skater gliding across the ice exemplifies this fluid integration of perception and response. As they execute each leap and spin, their awareness becomes one with the sensations of the blades against the frozen surface, the rush of air against their skin, and the rhythms of the accompanying music. The skater's body responds intuitively to the demands of the choreography without conscious deliberation.

Beyond artistic and athletic pursuits, the merging of action and awareness can also appear in more everyday contexts. A skilled chef, deeply absorbed in the preparation of a dish, may find that their movements flow seamlessly, guided by an intuitive understanding of the ingredients and cooking processes. A writer, fully immersed in the act of creation, may experience a state where words and ideas pour forth effortlessly, the boundary between the creator and the work dissolving in the process.

Back to my personal experience, during those initial cross-country skiing sessions, I acutely felt the disconnect between my intentions and my movements. I intellectually understood the techniques my instructor demonstrated—shifting weight from ski to ski, driving poles backward, maintaining forward momentum—yet consistently failed to translate that conceptual knowledge into embodied action. It seemed the harder I tried to consciously control my motions, the more entangled and resistant my skis became, stubbornly veering off-course at the slightest deviation in terrain.

But as I accumulated time on the snow, my nervous system began adapting to the subtle balance of forces required to navigate the environment efficiently. The rigid, mechanical motions gradually gave way to a more organic fluidity, each micro-adjustment arising seamlessly in response to the changing conditions. In those fleeting moments of grace, I even found myself gliding down the track effortlessly on one foot at times—a feat that amazed me with its cool, graceful mastery. The energy previously trapped in conscious thought transmuted into a palpable sense of oneness with the activity. Rather than deliberately plotting each step, movement flowed organically as an expression of unity with the surroundings, allowing me to manage hills and slopes with consistent, controlled speed.

3. Clear Goals

Flow thrives in contexts with clear, specific goals. Knowing precisely what we aim to achieve and receiving continuous input on our progress galvanizes attention and sustains focused engagement. In many sports, the overarching goals are unambiguous: traverse the course fastest, score the most points, and execute the most difficult routine. But even in more open-ended creative pursuits, framing our intentions with well-defined micro-goals can sharpen concentration and catalyze flow.

When it comes to Nordic skiing, goals exist at multiple levels. On a given outing, I might set an intention of completing a certain trail or logging a target distance. Within the actual rhythms of skiing, however, my focus telescopes to the momentary objectives necessitated by the terrain—maintaining speed through flat sections, transferring weight smoothly through turns, and finding the most efficient line up challenging inclines. The skis and poles provide instantaneous haptic and kinesthetic feedback, registering subtle errors in balance or power distribution as deviations in speed and trajectory.

This interplay of clearly defined targets creates a fertile ground for flow by dynamically steering attention and eliciting corrective adjustments in real time. The brain's orienting and executive networks lock into a rapid, reciprocal dialogue, allowing our responses to remain tightly coupled with the ever-changing environmental demands. Studies using neuroimaging have shown amplified activity in regions associated with goal-directed behavior and reward processing during flow states, including the prefrontal cortex, anterior cingulate cortex, and basal ganglia.

The amplified goal loop occupying our full attention leaves little mental bandwidth for abstract rumination and referential thought. The DMN responsible for mind-wandering grows quiet as we lose ourselves in the moment-by-moment unfolding of purposeful action.

However, even with clear objectives and tight feedback cycles establishing an environment conducive to flow, there were times when my body's needs would pull me out of that immersive state on the ski trails. When fatigue set in after extended periods of intense focus, I couldn't always get my physical movements to align with my intentions. Sometimes a quick break was required—a sip from my nutrient-primed water bottle and a brief rest would allow me to reset before continuing up that ominous hill ahead.

The flow experience wasn't a constant, unbroken experience, but rather something that would ebb and flow based on external factors like hydration levels, lack of sleep, or simply the accumulated stressors of the day. Yet each time I managed to re-enter that exhilarating zone of unselfconscious merging with the present-moment dynamics, I welcomed it with open arms. This resonates with my experience of falling in love with skate skiing. The technique was more challenging than classic skiing, but I found it infectious—I wanted to do it every time I hit the trails.

Despite the difficulty, or perhaps because of it, I was drawn into full engagement and presence. I later learned that the legendary mountaineer Anatoli Boukreev used skate skiing as his training for the incredible endurance demands of high-altitude climbing, reinforcing the idea that the clear objectives, immediate feedback, and optimal challenge of skate skiing create an ideal environment for cultivating flow and building mental and physical resilience (Boukreev, 2001).

While the periods of absorption may have been fleeting, those glimpses of flow reminded me to not get attached to sustaining the state indefinitely. Intentionally structuring the practice environment created more opportunities for flow to proliferate organically. But I learned to embrace the times it would inevitably dissolve, seeing each arising as a delicious fruit to be savored fully while it lasted, without clinging.

4. Unambiguous (Clear) Feedback

Equally essential for catalyzing flow is the ability to receive immediate, unambiguous feedback on our progress and performance. When we can continuously monitor our actions against clear informational cues from the environment, it becomes easier to course-correct in real time without interrupting our immersion.

On the ski trails, whether Nordic or Alpine, the primary feedback loop is a constant stream of tactile, kinesthetic, auditory, and visual information directly from my body's engagement with the activity. The skis themselves, along with the poles, provide an instantaneous haptic report on my technique, weight distribution, and power application through subtle deviations in speed, stability, and trajectory. The sound of the skis interacting with the snow offers additional data points. My proprioceptive awareness tracks the flow of subtle postural adjustments required to maintain balance and control.

In Nordic skiing specifically, this feedback loop is centered around the fundamental movements of push-off, weight transfer, and glide. As I balance on one foot, absorbing the terrain through ankle flexion and looking ahead, I'm constantly adjusting and readjusting in a continuous flow of motion.

This rich multisensory feedback loop allows me to remain hyperattuned and highly responsive to evolving conditions without having to pull back into analytical thought. I can make seamless microadjustments while staying absorbed in the present-moment dynamics rather than getting snagged by self-referential inner chatter.

However, even for an experienced skier, the value of external feedback should not be underestimated. Even after achieving advanced certifications, I still welcome insights from coaches observing and video analysis of my form. Their outside perspective allows me to continually refine areas of inefficiency and uncover blind spots in my technique that may go unnoticed by the internal feedback alone.

The combination of being attuned to the immediate multisensory feedback resonating through my body, while remaining open to purposeful critique from qualified external observers, creates an ideal feedback ecosystem for sustaining immersive flow experiences. It is this graceful "dance" of integrating both streams of feedback that enables ever-increasing levels of masterful skill and smoothness in skiing.

5. Concentration on the Task at Hand

Flow experiences are characterized by an intensely focused quality of attention, with mind–body resources devoted exclusively to the present moment's demands. Distractions—both internal and external—recede from awareness as our minds achieve an undivided absorption in the task. Whereas our ordinary consciousness frequently drifts between memories of the past, the anticipation of the future, and evaluations of the present, flow anchors us in a vivid immediacy. This unwavering concentration channels our full energy into skillfully responding to each fleeting instant.

As a beginner skier, my attention was scattered and porous—easily entrained by passing thoughts and environmental stimuli. I would find myself ruminating on a fall from twenty minutes prior, growing tense in anticipation of an approaching downhill, or comparing my halting movements to the fluidity of more experienced skiers. This diffuse, fractured quality of awareness made it difficult to enter flow, as my inner experience was only partially engaged with the living reality of the ski trails.

However, as my skills progressed and I tasted more glimpses of immersive concentration, my mind grew increasingly disciplined. I could intentionally let go of thoughts about the past or future and gently returning my focus to the sensory dimensions of skiing—the rush of cool air, the rhythmic swish of skis on snow, the lively burn of exertion in muscles—I learned to quiet distractions and unify attention in the present. The more fully I dedicated my awareness to the nuances of balance, speed, terrain, and technique, the more embodied flow began to spontaneously blossom.

As we learned in the section above, this heightened concentration in flow experiences is underpinned by a distinct pattern of neural activation and deactivation. Through deliberate practice, we can develop a facility for invoking this unified, undistracted quality of concentration in our chosen pursuits, amplifying our capacity for slipping into flow.

6. Paradox of Control

One of the hallmarks of flow is an empowering sense of effortless control over our actions and their consequences. Rather than feeling like a separate agent wrestling to impose our will on external circumstances, we experience a profound unity between intention, action, and outcome. Our movements and decisions seem to arise spontaneously and precisely when needed, elegantly adapting to the shifting constraints of the environment. This paradoxical feeling of control emerges not from clinging to a predetermined plan but from an egoless surrender to the intelligence of the moment.

Reflecting on my early forays into cross-country skiing, I recognize just how far my initial efforts were from this ideal. I clung to the poles with a white-knuckled grip, desperately trying to dictate every detail of my movements—the precise angle of the skis, the timing of each weight shift and kick, the force behind each pole plant. This grasping for control only bred resistance and frustration as I inevitably slipped, stumbled, and flailed.

As my skills developed, however, I learned to relax into a more responsive, improvisational relationship with the skis and terrain.

Relinquishing the need to micromanage my body, I instead relied on my internalized capacities to answer the challenges of the moment. This more flexible, resilient form of control—one rooted in sensitivity and attunement rather than predetermination and force—allowed me to dance with the changing landscape with greater ease and economy.

I recall one morning, gliding on one foot for longer than I thought possible, my attention captured by the fresh rabbit tracks crossing the newly fallen snow crystals. In that moment, I experienced a sense of effortless control, my body intuitively responding to the subtleties of the terrain, allowing me to fully immerse myself in the beauty of my surroundings. This sense of unity between intention, action, and outcome lies at the heart of the paradox of control in flow.

7. Loss of Reflective Self-Consciousness

Much of our waking mental experience is filtered through the lens of self-reflective awareness—a constant inner monologue evaluating our thoughts, emotions, and behaviors against an ingrained conceptual self-image. We relentlessly appraise ourselves through the memories of past experiences, deeply held beliefs about who we are, and the imagined judgments of others.

However, during flow experiences, this dualistic inner chatter fades into the background static as the firm boundaries between identity and activity begin to dissolve. The self's anxious ruminations over adequacy, flaws, and socially construed self-image grow faint and ultimately silent. Freed from the constant grip of the mind's inner chatter's nagging internal commentary, we can, at last, engage in our endeavors with unselfconscious abandon and spontaneous enthusiasm.

The mind unclenches from its withering contraction around a conceptual construct, allowing us to wholeheartedly immerse ourselves in the richness of present-moment sensations, challenges, and felt experiences unfolding around us. Unburdened by impression management, our gestures and responses arise with an ever-renewing freshness, fluidity, and presence. We become as artists on the canvas of reality itself—creative actors in the dynamic play of life.

Rather than a pinched, controlled performance stemming from mental rehearsal and second-guessing, our movements blossom as spontaneous celebratory expressions of attuned being. We soar beyond the psychic schism of subject and object, purposeful doer and conscious witness, reuniting in a trans-subjective experience of identity seamlessly merging with activity. In these rarified moments, the comforting shores of personhood are left behind as we surrender into the transforming mainstream of pure, unconditioned presence.

8. Transformation of Time

Among the most widely reported characteristics of flow is a warping of temporal perception. Our usual experience of time as a linear procession of discrete moments seems to melt and bend around the contours of our absorption. When we are utterly engrossed, hours can pass in what feels like the blink of an eye, while a few seconds may dilate into a subjective eternity.

As my relationship with Nordic skiing evolved, so too did my felt sense of time's passing. In those early days of struggle, when I was preoccupied with simply staying upright and avoiding catastrophe, time seemed to crawl by excruciatingly slow. A scant quarter-hour on the trails could feel like an endless, Sisyphean ordeal.

Yet once I honed my skills through dedicated practice, losing myself in the repetitions and nuances of technique mastery, my temporal awareness began slipping away entirely. I would ski along, utterly absorbed in exploring subtle adjustments of push off, weight shift, and gliding, only to be jolted by the realization that hours had dissolved in what felt like mere moments. On numerous occasions, I found myself having to set periodic timers, as I would completely lose track of how many laps I'd completed around the practice loop while immersed in the laser-focused work of refining each isolated movement.

Then, in those rare moments when everything crystallized—the skis, body, breath, and terrain unified in effortless resonance—the bondage of linear time would dissolve altogether and entire afternoons are eclipsed in a suspended eternity, an eternal present flowering across a vast, timeless expanse of direct embodied experiencing.

When I relaxed into this more integrated, flowing mode of being on my skis, the artificial constructs of past, present, and future began to peel away. My temporal reference points evaporated, leaving only the continuous unfolding of dynamically evolving sensations to inhabit and explore.

9. Autotelic Experience

Perhaps the defining quality of flow is its intrinsically rewarding nature. We pursue activities that elicit this state not for any external validation or gain, but for the sheer joy and fulfillment of the experience itself. The word *autotelic* translates from the Greek as "having its goal within itself" (Nakamura & Csikszentmihalyi, 2002). In flow, the act and its fruits are one and the same.

I believe many people may first approach Nordic skiing with a somewhat utilitarian mindset—a means to an end. It is a challenging yet efficient way to train balance and endurance during the winter season when preferred outdoor activities are limited—their motivations colored by a subtle instrumentality, as if banking "future capital" through the practice itself.

That said, this perspective began to change for me as I experienced more frequent and sustained flow on my skis. What started as a practical cross-training regimen revealed deeper layers of intrinsic reward. Those quiet hours gliding through hushed, snow-laden forests became increasingly alluring, not for any external outcome, but for the inherent nourishment and meaning they provided. Skiing transcended its initial role as a mere training tool and opened a gateway into the autotelic experience—an end in itself. The more I surrendered to the unbridled presence of flow, the more I recognized it not as a means to cultivate something else, but as the sublime embodiment and ultimate fruition of full, undivided participation itself.

Nevertheless, while each of the nine qualities was revealed distinctly through the challenges and breakthroughs of developing my Nordic skiing abilities, they also coalesced into an overarching cycle—an organic dance of integration and renewal.

Over the course of developing my Nordic skiing abilities, I experienced a gradual progression from beginner awkwardness and consciousness to increasing my embodied flow for that elusive glide. As my skills expanded to meet the challenges of more intermediate terrain, the mechanics of flexing ankles, shifting weight, and coordinating arm movements transitioned from conscious effort to a naturalistic merging of action and awareness.

I could negotiate trails with more fluid grace—getting in and out of tracks, avoiding collisions when yielding to others, and confidently descending winding hills with tight curves. However, this hard-earned flow was not a permanent state. Whenever conditions became too challenging, such as firm, icy snow or steeper, unfamiliar terrain, the cycle would reset. I found myself back in the beginner's mindset, needing to consciously relearn and re-embody the required techniques.

The disruption of flow didn't solely happen from increasing trail difficulty either. External factors like weather conditions, my current physical–mental state, or life stressors outside of skiing could all upset the delicate balance between challenge and skill. As authors like Brad Stulberg and Steve Magness outline in *Peak Performance*, growth emerges when we encounter moderate resistance that elevates our capabilities, but not so much that it induces burnout or shuts us down (Stulberg & Magness, 2017).

With an openness to revisiting mind–body, I could persistently re-enter realms of more embodied, unconscious engagement as the cycle repeated. The nine qualities became visceral lived experiences arising and dissolving in an organic dance—until the next integration of new skills at the edge of my abilities initiated the cycle anew.

Understanding the Science Behind Embodied Flow

Harnessing the power of flow can revolutionize our lives, but it demands a deep comprehension of the intricate brain dynamics during peak performance moments. Unraveling the neurological foundations and neurochemistry underlying embodied flow equips us with a potent toolkit to optimize performance and well-being. Equipped with this knowledge, we can intentionally craft environments, curate challenges, and train our minds to seamlessly access the zone.

But perhaps most importantly, this deeper comprehension of flow's neurological and neurochemical underpinnings allows us to reframe our perception of this practice. Rather than viewing it as an elusive or enigmatic phenomenon, we can embrace it as an inherent aspect of the human experience—a gift that each of us can access through the development of the right mindset and approach.

Neurological Basis of Embodied Flow

When we explore the neurological foundations of embodied flow, we discover a complex interplay of brain regions and neural networks that give rise to this transformative experience. One of the most striking findings is the profound shift in brain activity that occurs as we transition into flow.

Indeed, as you become fully immersed in an activity that challenges your skills and engages your attention, the prefrontal cortex—the part of your brain responsible for reflection, monitoring, and decision-making—begins to quiet down. This temporary silencing of the prefrontal cortex is known as transient hypofrontality, and it plays a crucial role in the flow experience.

With the chatter of the prefrontal cortex subdued, your mind enters into laser-focused attention, where all your mental resources are directed toward the task at hand. The constant stream of referential thoughts, doubts, and criticisms that often plague our waking consciousness fades into the background, allowing you to become one with the activity.

But while the prefrontal cortex takes a break, other brain regions kick into high gear. The parietal lobe, which handles all your sensory input and spatial awareness, gets super-activated. This heightened sensitivity allows you to tackle challenges with amazing precision and fluid grace.

Even if you're carving down a gnarly ski slope, your brain is working its tail off to take in all the information and guide your movements seamlessly. It's like your brain is doing overtime to help you perform at your peak in those intense moments.

Moreover, the cerebellum, a region crucial for coordinating motor skills and fine-tuning performance, also lights up during embodied flow. This enhanced cerebellar involvement contributes to the sense of effortless control and mastery that characterizes peak performance.

Recent research has also shed light on the role of brain wave synchronization in the flow experience. When fully absorbed in an activity, your brain waves tend to shift toward lower-frequency alpha and theta oscillations, particularly in the frontal and central regions. This synchronization facilitates the thorough integration of mind and body, allowing you to respond to challenges with intuitive ease and spontaneity.

Neurochemistry of Embodied Flow

The embodied-flow experience isn't just about brain regions and neural networks—it's also a neurochemical symphony that floods your system with feel-good compounds. During moments of intense engagement and optimal performance, your brain's reward centers light up like a Christmas tree.

A study by de Manzano et al. (2013) found that individuals with higher levels of dopamine in their brains were more likely to experience flow during challenging tasks. The researchers used positron-emission-tomography scans to measure dopamine levels and found that participants with greater dopamine release in the striatum, a key region involved in reward processing, reported more frequent and intense flow experiences.

Norepinephrine, a neurotransmitter that regulates arousal and attention, also surges during flow experience. Norepinephrine helps you stay alert and focused, allowing you to respond to the demands of the task with laser-like precision.

There is also the involvement of endorphins, the brain's natural pain relievers and mood elevators. As you push your mind and body to their limits during intense flow experiences, endorphins are released, creating a sense of euphoria and well-being that can persist long after the activity has ended. This explains why most long-distance runners exhibited increased levels of endorphins in their brains after completing a marathon. These endorphins not only helped them push through the pain and fatigue but also contributed to the great sense of accomplishment and joy that often accompanies flow experiences.

Furthermore, flow engagement may also be accompanied by increased levels of anandamide, an endogenous cannabinoid neurotransmitter. Anandamide, often referred to as the "bliss molecule," is associated with feelings of joy, relaxation, and expanded consciousness. Its presence during flow may contribute to boundless possibility and creative inspiration that often emerges in these peak moments.

Map the Neural Pathways for Optimal Performance

While the previous sections explored the overall neurological basis and neurochemistry involved in flow experiences, this section dives deeper into the intricate interplay between two specific neural networks—the DMN and the TPN.

By mapping out the roles of the DMN (associated with referential thought and mind-wandering) and the TPN (engaged when focusing externally on tasks), it illuminates the key neural dynamics that must be harmonized to achieve the immersive, hyperfocused embodied flow.

Essentially, this section reveals that entering embodied flow requires strategically downregulating the DMN to quiet the distracting inner monologue, while simultaneously upregulating the TPN to amplify task-focused attention, sensory integration, and precise execution.

Understanding this delicate neural balancing act and the higher-order control mechanisms that orchestrate it provides a neurological blueprint for the practical techniques and mindset shifts needed to embody flow on a sustainable basis.

Default Mode Network and Task-Positive Network

At the heart of the flow experience lies a delicate interplay between two fundamental neural networks: the DMN and the TPN. The DMN is a constellation of brain regions which include areas like the medial prefrontal cortex, posterior cingulate cortex, and angular gyrus. As previously mentioned, these regions become more active during referential thought, mind-wandering, and internal rumination.

When the DMN is highly active, we tend to experience mind-wandering, conscious thoughts, and a preoccupation with our internal mental chatter. This can be useful for reflection and contemplation, but it can also be a source of distraction and self-doubt, preventing us from fully immersing ourselves in the present moment.

In contrast, the TPN comprises brain regions that become more engaged when we direct our attention outward toward goal-oriented tasks and external stimuli. Key nodes of the TPN include the dorsolateral prefrontal cortex (involved in sustained attention and working memory), the intraparietal sulcus (responsible for processing sensory information and spatial awareness), and the supplementary motor area (which coordinates complex movements).

During our typical waking hours, the DMN and TPN engage in a dynamic balance, with one network becoming more active as the other deactivates. This ebb and flow between internal and external focus is a natural part of our daily experience.

However, in embodied flow, we see a unique and highly orchestrated pattern of activation and deactivation across these two networks. This shift in neural activity is crucial for enabling the exceptional levels of performance and immersive engagement that characterize flow experiences.

Balancing the DMN and TPN for Embodied Flow

To embody flow, your brain needs to strike a delicate balance between the DMN and TPN. Neuroimaging studies reveal that as individuals transition into flow, specific regions within the DMN, such as the ventromedial prefrontal cortex and posterior cingulate cortex, exhibit decreased activity. This reduction in the DMN's referential processing is akin to hitting a "mute button" on your inner critic, allowing you to quiet the incessant chatter of doubts and conscious thoughts.

Concurrently, key nodes of the TPN become highly integrated and activated, orchestrating a symphony of cognitive resources. This enables high focus, seamless integration of sensory information, and precise execution of complex movements.

Pragmatically speaking, this delicate balancing act between the DMN and TPN is not a passive byproduct of the flow experience. Instead, it is an active, top-down process orchestrated by higher-order cognitive control mechanisms, particularly the dorsolateral prefrontal cortex.

As we'll explore in depth later in this book, cultivating present-moment awareness through mindfulness can quiet the referential chatter of the DMN, allowing the TPN to take center stage and direct cognitive resources toward the task at hand. We'll dive even deeper into the transformative potential of mindfulness in Chapter 2, where I'll guide you through specific techniques for embodying this state of conscious presence.

Chapter 2:

Mindful Movement

In our previous exploration of flow's neurological foundations, we saw that achieving this rarified state of peak performance requires quieting the DMN associated with incessant referential chatter, while simultaneously activating the TPN governing outward attentiveness and seamless mind–body coordination.

Theoretical understanding alone, however, is not enough to induce this neural harmonization. We must implement specialized training practices that can directly repattern and synchronize the DMN and TPN networks. This is where the path of mindful embodiment comes in.

Kelly Slater, an 11-time world champion surfer, is a great example of how important it is to consistently practice mindfulness. When I dug deeper, I realized that Slater's rock-solid commitment to these practices has been the backbone of his unparalleled success. It's the reason he's been able to stay at the top of his game for more than two decades, constantly redefining what's possible in the world of surfing.

Central to Slater's regimen is his daily breath work and meditation routine. He begins each morning with an extended sequence of conscious breathing exercises, which uses patterned inhalations and exhalations paired with cold exposure to induce profound psychophysiological coherence.

When he methodically cycles his breath in this way, Slater is able to downregulate his mind's persistent narrative loop and anxiety patterning. This allows him to access unconstrained present-moment awareness—exactly the open, unconscious attunement required for the TPN to harmoniously engage during competition.

In the tumultuous arena of professional surfing, this embodied mindfulness unveils itself as Slater's preternatural ability to read and preemptively sync with the ocean's perpetually shifting geometries. While most competitors struggle to cognitively grasp the wave's dynamics, Slater's decoupling from fixated thought allows him to fluidly merge with its very forces as they arise.

During competitions, observers describe Slater's being as seemingly indistinguishable from the wave's motion itself. He ceases effortful "doing" and instead rides the intensifying emergent with a poet surfer's liquid grace. This capacity for existential mind–body flow is what has allowed him to not just defeat the world's greatest wave riders consistently since the 1990s, but to innovate completely new maneuvers that redefined the sport's possibilities.

From his invention of the seamless "Slater spin" aerial technique to his ability to emerge unscathed from wipeouts that would likely kill most people, Slater's prowess stems directly from this intensive cross-training of embodied mindfulness. Due to his commitment to a lifestyle of nervous system repatterning through breath work, meditation, and immersive nature reconnection, he has optimized his psychobiological processing for present-moment absorption.

Of course, Slater's mindfulness work is just one aspect of his remarkably balanced, holistic approach to training, but there's no denying that his embodied-flow mindset is what sets him apart.

Embodying the Flow Code: Training Mindful Movement

The path of mindful embodiment involves systematically upgrading our psychobiological operating system for peak performance. Just as we consciously train physical attributes like strength, endurance, and flexibility, these practices provide an analogous methodology for expanding our perceptual bandwidth, focused attention, and mind–body integration.

For too long, our cultural conditioning has indoctrinated a mindset of attempting to "control" our state of being solely through the force of conscious will. We berate ourselves for lacking motivation or discipline when aspirations fail to manifest. Yet this paradigm represents a profound disconnection from the deeper wisdom of unified consciousness flowing through our beings.

The flow's experts have revealed that rather than white-knuckling our way toward excellence, true embodied genius arises through intentionally relaxing the mind's suppressive grasp. By systematically rewiring reflexive thought/behavior patterns, we can effectively update our psychobiological "core programming" to harmonize with the unfolding present moment.

This is the essence of mindful movement—not only physical training but also a holistic repatterning of our perceptual reality itself. Through somatic practices like breath work, meditation, and felt-sense reconditioning, we're able to progressively unshackle ourselves from the limiting cycles of adaptive narratives. Layers of cognitive conditioning, emotional reactivity, and unconsciously held muscular bracing begin to shed as we reconnect with our intrinsic embodied flow.

From this space of open, relaxed presence, our innate responsiveness and sensitivity can align with the world in profound coherence. We become like world-class artists, spontaneously expressing the perfect action for any given scenario as it occurs—whether that's an elite athlete mirroring their environment with seemingly superhuman reaction times or an entrepreneur navigating ever-shifting market forces with preternatural leadership intuition.

Essentially, mindful movement trains us to no longer exist armored in the conceptual trance of assumed selfhood. The well-trodden grooves of fear, attachment, and separateness that many people sleepwalk through life in begin to release their grip. In their place, an unconditioned field of unified perception blossoms—the same state of unified flow that great masters across disciplines have embodied.

So, while the specific techniques of breath work, visualization, proprioceptive recalibration, and more represent the training tools, the essence of mindful embodiment is far more transformative. It's about progressively transcending our human conditioning to experience life not as a disjointed series of narrative-driven circumstances, but as a unified field of cocreative participation. With commitment, the practices hollow out space for our innate wholeness to emerge— catalyzing the next stage of human potential.

From this vantage, the methodologies are not solely about optimizing performance in the conventional sense. They're *portkeys* into awakening as continuously individuated expressions of the same eternal continuum. Each intentional breath, each reconnection with our kinesthetic felt-sensations, and each quiet moment of centered presence undermines the antiquated legacy programming keeping us bound to the sleepwalk of separateness.

With this context, let's now explore some of the foundational techniques.

Conscious Breath Work

The breath is our innate biorhythm—a constantly unfolding process that interlaces and entrains the conscious and unconscious realms. As we attune our awareness to this eternal ebb and flow, we begin to unravel the knots of dissonance that bind our mind–body in discordant frequencies. Through the breath, we find harmony in the chaos, a symphony of psychophysiological unity.

Dr. Andrew Weil's elegantly simple 4-7-8 breathing technique provides an accessible on-ramp for cultivating this mind–body synchronization. This purposeful breathing pattern signals the body's parasympathetic nervous system (which governs rest, digestion, and relaxation) to downshift from sympathetic fight-or-flight arousal (the stress response governed by the sympathetic nervous system) into a physiological state primed for relaxed yet focused awareness (Weil, 2016).

To practice the 4-7-8 breath work method

1. Sit upright, softening your gaze or gently closing your eyes.

2. Exhale fully through slightly pursed lips, producing a soft "whooosh" from your diaphragm.

3. With your mouth closed, silently inhale through your nose to a mental count of 4.

4. Hold this inhale for a count of 7.

5. Exhale fully again through pursed lips to a count of 8, releasing with a "whooosh."

Repeat this cyclical pattern 4–8 times shortly after waking each morning and once more in the evening before bed. The specific inhalation–pause–exhalation ratio helps reset your autonomic nervous system baseline by reducing synthesized stress hormones like cortisol while simultaneously activating neurochemical and physiological markers correlated with inner stillness and presence.

As you consistently integrate this potent yet simple breath work practice into your routine, you'll likely begin noticing a pervasive heightening of embodied presence and mindful clarity infusing your daily experience and activities. Physical holding patterns may soften, emotions can feel more coherent and integrated, and your capacity to remain centered amidst turbulence will progressively expand. This signals the commencement of that crucial psychosomatic reintegration and harmonization.

While the 4-7-8 breathing technique can provide great benefits on its own, it also represents an accessible entry point into more immersive breath work modalities. As you become intimately attuned to the anchoring rhythm of your breath, you can build upon this foundation by layering complementary techniques like coherence breathing, heart breathing, holotropic breath work, and more.

Even just 5–10 minutes of conscious breath work integrated into your daily routine can catalyze profound repatterning and upgrades in mind–body attunement over time. It's an incredibly potent yet remarkably simple and pragmatic catalyst for optimizing psychophysiological coherence and flow capabilities.

Psychologists and breath work specialists like Dr. Patricia Gerbarg, Dr. Richard Brown, and Dan Brulé have extensively researched and mapped the physiological mechanisms underpinning the benefits of purposeful breathing practices like 4-7-8. Their research shows how entraining extended exhalation ratios can modulate oxytocin, vasopressin, and other neuropeptides integrally involved in activating the parasympathetic "rest and digest" autonomic system.

This downregulation of sympathetic nervous system arousal then allows the body to conserve metabolic resources and reallocate them toward enhancing heart rate variability, vagal tone, and frontal brain asymmetry patterns associated with states of mindful presence, emotional regulation, and heightened perception.

So in layman's terms, conscious breathing quite literally rewires and optimizes your psychobiological operating system for flow by harmonizing the mind–body feedback loops between conscious awareness and autonomic functioning. It's an elegant, accessible avenue into embodied presence.

Dr. Belisa Vranich, a respected researcher and breath work teacher, has pioneered research showing that controlled, patterned breathing can quickly alter brain wave activity and neurotransmitter production. These changes enhance neuroplasticity, emotional regulation, and higher cognitive functions such as creativity and fluid intelligence, supporting the idea that the breath is a powerful tool for improving our overall mind–body well-being (Vranich, 2020).

For sure, breath work is just one dimension of an integrated journey into mindful embodiment. But it provides an invaluable entry point into awakening our somatic intelligence and harmonizing our conscious and subconscious psychophysiological processing. With committed practice, it can unlock profound upgrades in our innate flow capacities.

Visualization

The visualization's power to upgrade our mind–body coherence and access flow is supported by pioneering research in neuroscience and psychology. One prime example comes from the work of Dr. Stephen

Porges, the developer of the polyvagal theory. His studies demonstrate how clearly generating imagery of felt-sense experiences like safety, connection, and reciprocity can directly modulate the neural pathways governing our autonomic nervous system responses (Porges, 2011).

In simpler terms, when we use multisensory visualization to imagine realistic experiences that make us feel calm, secure, and attuned with our environment, we can consciously "rewire" the subconscious threat responses that tend to derail us from flow. Visualization allows us to signal safety to our brain's evolutionary "defense" wiring so we can stay in an integrated mind–body experience.

Activating Your Visionary Intelligence

To begin integrating visualization into your embodiment practice, try this simple exercise:

1. Sit comfortably and bring your awareness fully into the present moment through a few deep breaths.

2. Call to mind a time when you felt completely relaxed, safe, and at ease—perhaps on a beach vacation or tucked in bed as a child.

3. Don't just recall the visual scene, but use all your senses to vividly reexperience those somatic textures of peacefulness: the smells, the warm sunlight on your skin, and the sounds of the environment.

4. Sustain this immersive remembrance for 2–3 minutes, breathing slowly and continuously refreshing the details.

This helps activate your mind's capacity to richly imagine and viscerally inhabit a desired psychophysiological experience, which is key for advanced visualization work.

Building on this foundation, more complex visualization practices have been developed and studied in sports psychology and performance optimization fields. These techniques often involve detailed, multisensory mental rehearsal of desired skills or peak experiences (Roychowdhury, 2023).

Advanced Visualization Techniques

To practice advanced visualization for your chosen field

1. Begin with a few minutes of conscious breathing to center yourself.

2. Vividly imagine yourself in an immersive situation where you're flawlessly demonstrating the skill, ability, or peak experience you wish to cultivate.

3. Don't just passively watch, but embody the experience through all your senses. What do you perceive around you? What are the specific felt-sense details of being in that "zone"?

4. Sustain this vivid multisensory immersion for 5–10 minutes, making the details as rich as possible.

For example, if you're an athlete, you might envision hearing the crowd's roar as you step into the arena, seeing the glistening court beneath your feet, and feeling your body move with preternatural grace as you compete at the highest level. If you're an entrepreneur, imagine the avenues of success—hearing the excitement from investors as you pitch your vision, feeling the energy of the room as you speak with charisma and confidence.

Or, if you're a paraglider pilot, visualize yourself gliding through the sky, feeling the wind against your face, and intuitively navigating the currents as you gracefully maneuver your glider. Imagine the breathtaking vista below you, the sense of freedom and exhilaration coursing through your body, and the complete sense of unity in three-dimensional space as you fly.

The more realistically you can pre-live these heightened experiences, the more effectively you're priming your psychobiological instrument to naturally embody them in reality.

In terms of case studies exemplifying this process, we can look at elite athletes who have relied on visualization to propel their skills into rarified flow performances:

- Three-time Olympic gold medalist visualization pioneer Lanny Bassham adopted disciplined visualization to meticulously pre-experience every possible scenario in his rifle shooting competitions. By specifically running through flawless performances in his mind's eye hundreds of times, he was able to radically upgrade his embodied-flow experiences on the firing line.

- World-class professional golfers like Tiger Woods and Jack Nicklaus leveraged detailed course visualization well before every tournament round—vividly feeling the curves and reads of each green from every conceivable angle and lie. This pre-encoding allowed them to automatically tap into an intimate full-body knowing when they stepped onto those greens in peak moments.

- Gymnasts like Olga Korbut and Nadia Comeneci employed extensive visualization of their full routines from a somatic first-person perspective, feeling the rotational dynamics and seamlessly perfect executions many times before stepping onto the competition floor. This enabled them to fully embody the most challenging stunt sequences as second-nature flow expressions.

The science is clear—disciplined multisensory visualization has the capacity to progressively harmonize our psychobiological instrument and optimize us for accessing flow on demand, regardless of our performance arena. World-class athletes have long used it as a secret catalyst for pushing into new realms of mastery.

Most impressively, just by combining visualization with breath work, conscious movement arts, and immersive situational rehearsal, we can rapidly evolve into fully coherent beings sustaining creativity, peak performance, and flow as a natural way of being. And with committed practice attuning our perception to these subtle interior resonances, we shed the conventional blinders of cultural and human limitation, awakening as radiant masterworks of dynamic expression, our inner and outer worlds unified in a continual unfolding of realized potential.

Proprioception

Often referred to as "the sixth sense," proprioception is our innate capacity to attune to the subtlest feelings of position, movement, and visceral aliveness coursing through our beings.

In our modern culture of disembodied abstraction, most of us have severely atrophied this psychophysiological bandwidth—essentially experiencing life through a filtered conceptual narrative disconnected from raw sensorial reality. We move and act while cut off from the nonverbal wisdom pulsing through our flesh and neuromuscular dynamics.

Awakening and refining proprioceptive acuity are essential for harmonizing the mind–body connection into peak coherence. And like any embodied skill, proprioceptive intelligence can be systematically developed through dedicated somatic practices.

Building Your Proprioceptive Foundation

One of the most pioneering systems for developing proprioception is the Feldenkrais Method. Created by Dr. Moshé Feldenkrais (1972), it uses gentle movement sequences and guided attention practices to upgrade sensory acuity and kinesthetic awareness.

A foundational Feldenkrais exercise is a seated spinal rotation:

1. Sit upright on the front edge of a chair, feet flat on the floor.

2. Gently rotate your upper body to the right, allowing your gaze to follow the turn without forcing it.

3. Notice the symphony of subtle sensation—the shifting weight, the torsions, the internal landscapes.

4. Pause, then slowly rotate back through the center and to the left side, maintaining panoramic bodily attention.

5. Repeat this full rotation 5–10 times at a relaxed, exploratory pace.

Already, you're engaging your proprioceptive field in a new way—not by straining into positions, but by becoming a richly attuned witness to the sensations naturally arising.

To build further embodied presence, try this Feldenkrais-inspired micromovement:

1. Stand with feet hip-width apart, arms relaxed at your sides.

2. Gently bend your knees as you inhale, allowing your spine to naturally arch slightly back.

3. As you exhale, pivot your weight onto one leg as the other begins to extend behind you into a mini-lunge.

4. With each breath cycle, slowly alternate extending the opposite leg behind—all while softly directing your gaze through the subtle shifts.

Explore this meditative movement for 5–10 cycles, refining your sensitivity to the streaming interplay of forces, trajectories, and kaleidoscopic textures within.

Embodying Through Motion

For a more advanced proprioceptive challenge, you can try this coordinated movement exercise:

1. Standing tall, simultaneously circle your arms outward while circling one knee outward.

2. Pause and reverse the arm circles as you circle the opposite knee outward.

3.   Now try opposing circles—one knee outward as the arms circle inward.

4.   Repeat these patterned sequences for one-minute intervals, ceiling your interior awareness through the intricate coordinative spirals.

Practices like these initiate the unraveling of unconscious holding patterns and conditioned movement habits, helping you reclaim an unbounded proprioceptive repertoire.

To amplify your kinesthetic awakening, incorporate daily motion-based meditation

1.   Set a timer for a duration that feels manageable to you, whether it's 1 minute, 3 minutes, 5 minutes, or longer.

2.   With no set routine, simply move spontaneously in any organic way—perhaps beginning with subtle sways, bends, or spiral initiations.

3.   Use the breath to soundtrack your unfolding exploration on the present moment's impulses.

4.   Whenever you find fixation arising, consciously dissolve back into organic fluidity.

5.   Simply inhabit and bear witness to the ever-shifting landscapes of living sensation within.

Remember, don't get hung up on trying to force a particular form. Just tune your conscious mind into the ever-shifting proprioceptive rhythms.

Sustaining the Practice

As you integrate these exercises over weeks and months, you'll experience thoughtful openings. Once-suppressed strata of somatic intelligence decompressing. Physical blockages evaporating. A reclaiming of unbounded proprioceptive radiance.

To expedite these unfurlings, complement your practices with sound baths, myofascial unwinding sessions, or any somatic immersions that initiate reunification with your primal kinesthetic genius.

The most crucial element? An eagerness to approach this somatic terrain with infinite awe, curiosity, and patience. For within the subtlest textures pulsing through your sacred vessel lie cosmic codes beckoning your soulful remembering as a vibrational maestro.

When you finally surrender to this cellular renaissance, life itself becomes your magnum opus—a resonant flowing of virtuosic creativity emerging from unbounded proprioceptive absorption in the infinite present. All actions, decisions, and exchanges arise as pristine verses in an eternal masterwork symphony exquisitely improvised just for you.

Just as Kelly Slater's firm commitment to embodied mindfulness has allowed him to redefine the boundaries of what's possible in surfing, your own dedication to these practices can unlock uncharted realms of potential in your chosen craft and your life. The path of mindful embodiment is an ever-unfolding journey of discovery, inviting you to dive deeper into the boundless ocean of your being with each passing moment.

Chapter 3:

Finely Tuning the Athletic Body for

Embodying Flow

The power of the mind and body working in harmonious unity is what truly unleashes extraordinary potential. While embodied focus and determination are crucial, they must be coupled with a finely tuned physical instrument that can respond fluidly to the demands of peak performance. You cannot optimize the mind or body in isolation— they are an interconnected system that requires integrated conditioning to achieve an embodied-flow experience.

The body–mind's aspirations are nothing without a body tuned as a responsive, experience-filled instrument. Conversely, a remarkable physical instrument loses its potency without the governing force of embodied focus and awareness. Only when the mind–body is developed as an interdependent, synced system can one fully embody a flow experience and unleash its innate creative and performance capabilities.

This integrated mind–body approach is increasingly being validated by cutting-edge research across various elite performance domains, from endurance sports to the extremes of human potential.

I've seen how the tiniest tweaks in nutrition, recovery, and training can make the difference between a personal best and a DNF. Take the work of Dr. Stacy Sims, an exercise physiologist shaking up the field with her research on tailoring nutrition and training to the physiology of female athletes. Her book *ROAR* provides practical strategies for optimizing factors like hydration and nutrient timing to support hormonal demands, helping athletes solve issues like fatigue and bonking (Sims, 2016).

Then there's the groundbreaking work of Dr. Marcus Elliott's P3 Applied Sports Science team. They've developed a sophisticated system for assessing biomechanical efficiency, pinpointing imbalances, and designing targeted programs to optimize movement and reduce injury risk (P3 - Peak Performance Project, 2021). Athletes utilizing their approach experience breakthroughs by tapping into their full biomechanical potential.

A prime example of Dr. Elliott's approach in action is the case of NFL quarterback Tom Brady. After undergoing a comprehensive biomechanical assessment at P3, Brady identified specific areas of improvement in his throwing mechanics. The P3 team then designed a targeted training program to optimize his movement efficiency and reduce the risk of injury. As a result, Brady experienced a significant increase in his throwing velocity and accuracy as well as improved overall performance and career longevity.

But perhaps one of the most compelling examples of the body's incredible capacity for adaptation and performance comes from the world of extreme sports.

Take someone like Wim Hof, the "Iceman" who's famous for his superhuman feats of endurance in sub-zero temperatures. Through a combination of specialized breathing techniques, cold exposure training, and sheer mental fortitude, Hof has demonstrated an astonishing ability to consciously control his autonomic nervous system and immune response. He's even been injected with endotoxins under medical supervision and shown the ability to completely neutralize their inflammatory effects through the power of his breath and concentration. If that's not a testament to the untapped potential of the human body, I don't know what is.

But you don't have to be a world-class athlete or a freak of nature to start harnessing the incredible adaptability and resilience of your own physiology. Simply implement some straightforward science-backed principles and learn to listen closely to your body signals, you can start the process of fine-tuning your own performance, one small change at a time.

In addition to paying attention to those subtle signals and responding with nurturing adjustments to your nutrition, movement, and recovery routines, you'll gradually experience a considerable transformation. Just as a skilled pianist meticulously tunes their instrument, each small tweak and refinement will bring you closer to a state of exquisite harmony and balance.

And the best part? As you optimize your mind–body's functioning, you start to feel increasingly vital and capable in your own skin—that sense of physical empowerment can't help but spill over into every other area of your life. When you know that you have the energy, strength, and resilience to tackle any challenge that comes your way, it frees up so much mind–body bandwidth to focus on the things that really light you up.

So, as we dive into the nitty-gritty of physical optimization in the pages to come, I invite you to approach the process with a sense of wonder, playfulness, and discovery. Treat your mind–body as the incredible gift and ally that it is, and let yourself get swept up in the joy of exploring its hidden potential. Trust me—you'll be amazed at just how much your remarkable embodied peak experience is truly capable of achieving.

Optimizing Embodied Peak Performance

This section explores the critical role of optimizing the body's physical alignment, function, and performance in achieving peak athletic results. We dive into the fundamental principles of sports nutrition, periodization and structured training cycles, and the importance of rest and recovery.

Fueling the Body

From the intense, explosive power of Olympic weightlifters to the incredible endurance of ultramarathon runners, one common thread emerges: a deep understanding of how to optimally fuel their bodies for the unique demands of their discipline.

Nutrition Principles

The foundation of any successful fueling strategy lies in a solid grasp of fundamental nutrition principles. At the most basic level, our bodies require a precise balance of macronutrients (carbohydrates, proteins, and fats) and micronutrients (vitamins and minerals) to function at their peak.

Carbohydrates, the body's preferred fuel source for high-intensity efforts, are critical for maintaining energy levels and preventing fatigue during training and competition. The recommended daily carbohydrate intake is based on body weight and activity type (Burke et al., 2011):

- Endurance athletes: 2.3–3.2 g/lb/day (5–7 g/kg/day)

- Shorter, high-intensity activities: 1.4–2.3 g/lb/day (3–5 g/kg/day)

To calculate your daily carbohydrate needs, multiply your body weight in pounds by the appropriate factor above. For example, a 150-lb (68-kg) endurance athlete would aim for approximately 345–480 g of carbohydrates per day (150 lb x 2.3–3.2 g/lb/day).

In addition to the daily carbohydrate intake based on body weight, endurance athletes engaging in activities lasting longer than an hour may need to consume additional carbohydrates during the activity to maintain performance and delay fatigue. The general recommendation is to consume 30–60 g of easily digestible carbs per hour of continuous exercise lasting more than 1 hour. This is not a replacement for the daily carbohydrate intake but rather a supplementary strategy to support performance during prolonged endurance activities.

Protein is essential for supporting muscle repair, growth, and adaptation. Aim for 1.2 to 2.0 g of protein per kg of body weight, depending on the intensity and type of activity. High-quality protein sources like grass-fed beef, wild-caught fish, free-range eggs, and plant-based options like quinoa and tempeh should be a staple of any athlete's diet (Thomas et al., 2016).

Within 30 minutes post-workout, consume a combination of fast-absorbing whey protein along with a source of easily digestible carbs like a banana to promote optimal muscle synthesis and recovery. You can also blend the whey protein with the banana and leafy greens like spinach for added nutrients and fiber to aid absorption.

Healthy fats play a crucial role in hormone production, nutrient absorption, and sustained energy. The general recommendation for fat intake is 20%–35% of your daily calories from healthy fats, such as avocados, nuts, seeds, olive oil, and fatty fish. Omega-3 fatty acids are particularly beneficial for reducing inflammation and supporting overall health.

However, it's crucial to emphasize that women's bodies tend to be more efficient at burning fat for fuel compared to men. This is due to various factors, including hormonal differences and body composition. As a result, some women may benefit from consuming a slightly higher percentage of their daily calories from healthy fats, potentially up to 40% in some cases.

For example, if a woman consuming 2,000 calories per day aims for 35%–40% of her calories from fat, she would need to consume 78–89 g of fat per day (2,000 calories x 0.35–0.40 ÷ 9 calories per g of fat).

It's best to focus on consuming healthy fats from whole-food sources and to limit the intake of saturated and trans fats, which are associated with negative health outcomes.

Nonetheless, individual macronutrient requirements can vary significantly. Factors such as body composition, training intensity, and personal physiology heavily influence the optimal balance of carbohydrates, proteins, and fats.

In my experience as a lean athlete, I've found that my body functions best on a higher percentage of carbohydrates and a lower percentage of fat compared to the general recommendations. However, arriving at this understanding was a journey of trial and error. It took time and experimentation to figure out what worked best for my unique physiology, as I didn't fit neatly into the norms or research findings.

That's why I wholeheartedly encourage you to seek out the guidance of experienced nutritional and workout coaches who can help you deal with this complex landscape. They will work with you to fine-tune your macronutrient ratios, optimize your fueling strategies, and emphasize the importance of nutrient-dense, whole-food choices. Surely, this personalized approach is nothing short of transformative.

Individual Metabolism and Physiology

An athlete's unique metabolism and physique play a significant role in their nutritional requirements. Factors such as body composition, muscle mass, and resting metabolic rate can influence the amount of energy an athlete needs to consume to maintain optimal performance and recovery. Understanding how individual physiology responds to various nutrients and training stimuli is key to tailoring a fueling strategy that supports an athlete's specific goals and needs.

However, given the numerous factors that can influence an athlete's nutritional needs, such as age, gender, body composition, and specific training routines, it's crucial to approach this topic with caution and avoid overgeneralizing. The complexities of individualized nutrition strategies make it difficult to provide one-size-fits-all recommendations that apply to all athletes.

Instead, athletes should consider seeking guidance from a certified nutritional coach who can help them develop personalized strategies tailored to their unique needs and goals. Keeping a detailed journal of dietary intake, training sessions, and performance metrics can provide valuable insights for adjusting an athlete's fueling plan in collaboration with their coach.

Optimal daily fueling for both endurance and strength athletes involves spreading nutrient intake throughout the day to support energy levels, promote recovery, and maintain a healthy body composition. Athletes should aim to consume balanced meals and snacks that contain a mix of carbohydrates, proteins, and healthy fats every 3–4 hours to keep blood sugar levels stable and provide a steady supply of nutrients to working muscles. The specific timing and amount of nutrient intake in relation to training and competition may vary depending on the individual athlete, the duration and intensity of the workout, and the goals of the training session.

To further explore this topic, I highly recommend Dr. Marc Bubbs' (2019) book, *Peak: The New Science of Athletic Performance That Is Revolutionizing Sports*, which will be listed in the reference section at the end of this book. Dr. Bubbs, a naturopathic doctor and performance nutrition expert, offers evidence-based insights on optimizing nutrition for various types of athletes while emphasizing the importance of individualization and professional guidance.

Hydration for Peak Performance

But even the most perfectly calibrated macronutrient balance can be derailed by poor hydration. Intense training can lead to rapid fluid and electrolyte losses through sweat, leading to decreased performance, impaired cognitive function, and even dangerous conditions like heat illness if left unchecked.

Athletes should drink enough fluids throughout the day to maintain pale, straw-colored urine and replace sweat losses during exercise. The American College of Sports Medicine recommends that athletes drink 16–20 oz (475–590 ml) of fluid 4 hours before exercise, 8–12 oz (235–355 ml) 10–15 minutes before exercise, and 3–8 oz (90–235 ml) every 15–20 minutes during exercise, depending on individual sweat rates and the intensity and duration of the activity (Sawka et al., 2007). Again, I have to mention that these are general guidelines, and individual hydration needs may vary based on factors such as body size, sweat rate, and environmental conditions.

It's not just about consuming fluids; it's about consuming the right fluids. So, avoid excessive caffeine, sugars, or alcohol, which can contribute to dehydration. The ideal hydration strategy includes a balanced intake of electrolytes like sodium, chloride, potassium, calcium, and magnesium to replace what's lost through sweat.

While staying hydrated is essential, it's also important to avoid overhydration, which can lead to a dangerous condition called hyponatremia (low blood sodium levels). This can occur when athletes consume excessive amounts of fluids, particularly low-electrolyte fluids like plain water, and don't replace the electrolytes lost through sweat.

To take hydration to the next level, athletes can develop individualized hydration plans based on their sweat rate and composition. This level of personalization is a game-changer. Rather than relying on generic, one-size-fits-all hydration advice, we can pinpoint the precise amount and type of fluids an athlete needs to consume to stay on top of their game. In the world of elite performance, these tiny details can make all the difference.

The type of activity and environmental conditions further influence an athlete's unique fueling needs. In hot and humid conditions, athletes should prioritize fluid and electrolyte replacement to counteract increased sweat losses and maintain core body temperature. This may involve consuming sports drinks or electrolyte supplements before, during, and after the event, and adjusting fluid intake based on individual sweat rates and the intensity and duration of the activity.

At high altitudes, athletes may experience decreased appetite, increased respiratory water losses, and altered digestion and absorption of nutrients. To support optimal performance and adaptation to altitude, athletes should focus on consuming easily digestible, nutrient-dense foods, staying hydrated with electrolyte-rich fluids, and allowing sufficient time for acclimatization before competing. If you're a high-altitude climber, additional strategies are crucial. Increasing dietary fat intake, especially at night, helps provide extra insulating calories to maintain warmth in extreme cold conditions. Consuming high-fat foods and drinks maximizes energy density when appetite is suppressed at altitude.

Regarding cold temperatures, athletes may be at risk of dehydration due to reduced thirst sensation and increased respiratory water losses. To maintain fluid balance and support optimal performance, athletes should make a conscious effort to drink fluids regularly, even if they don't feel thirsty, and consume warm, hydrating beverages like tea or broth to promote vasodilation and maintain core body temperature.

Nevertheless, individual physiology and nutritional needs are not static; they can change over time due to factors such as aging, stress, overuse, or injury. Monitoring these needs is an art in itself, requiring careful attention and ongoing adjustments. Athletes should work closely with sports nutritionists and other healthcare professionals to reassess their nutritional requirements periodically and make appropriate modifications to their fueling strategies. By staying attuned to their body's evolving needs and adapting their approach accordingly, athletes can ensure they are always optimally fueled for their unique demands and goals.

For an inspiring look at how rewriting one's relationship with food can unlock new levels of performance, I frequently point to the trail-blazing career of Jessie Diggins.

Diggins etched her name into sporting immortality by becoming the first American to win Olympic gold in cross-country skiing, achieving this historic triumph in the women's team sprint at the 2018 Pyeongchang Games alongside her teammate Kikkan Randall. This monumental victory marked a significant milestone for U.S. cross-country skiing.

But this crowning achievement was just the beginning. Diggins' relentless pursuit of excellence saw her conquering new heights. She continued to excel on the world stage, claiming the overall World Cup title in the 2020–2021 season, making her the first American to achieve this feat. Her journey from that historic Olympic moment to becoming the world's best has been an incredible tale of grit, resilience, and the hard-won ability to sync body and mind in the relentless pursuit of greatness.

However, Diggins's journey to the top was not without its challenges!

In her candid memoir *Brave Enough*, Diggins pulls back the curtain on her years-long battle with bulimia—an eating disorder characterized by cycles of binge eating followed by purging (Diggins & Smith, 2020). The disorder first took root during her teenage years, with Diggins vividly recounting the overwhelming shame, guilt, and loathing that would consume her after eating. This sparked a destructive cycle of excessive exercise and purging behaviors as she desperately tried to regain control, nearly derailing her promising skiing career.

Determined to overcome her struggles, Diggins embarked on a journey to rewrite her relationship with food and her body. She found inspiration in Dr. Stacy Sims' book *ROAR*, which emphasizes tailoring nutrition to female athletes' unique physiology. Drawing from resources like Sims's work, Diggins could implement a cyclical nutritional approach that aligned with her menstrual cycle.

Diggins's new nutrition plan centered on wholesome foods like fruits, whole grains, lean meats, and plant-based proteins, with a strong emphasis on proper hydration. In her own words, "I truly believe that if you can enjoy all types of foods in moderation, you never feel like you're withholding anything from yourself, and you're not tempted to go nuts on whatever food you've deemed 'off-limits'" (Mast, 2024).

To support her rigorous training and racing demands, Diggins also developed a strategic fueling approach. She's diligent about consuming a mix of carbohydrates and protein within 30 minutes post-workout to optimize recovery. Even during grueling sessions when hunger cues may be suppressed, Diggins ensures adequate fueling to maintain energy levels and prevent overtraining.

"You won't always feel hungry during a workout, especially if you're running or going hard," she explains. "I always have snacks with me, and I make sure to eat them even if I'm not particularly excited about it" (Diggins, 2020).

Diggins also sought support from therapists and worked with the Emily Program, a renowned eating disorder treatment center. Through open, honest conversations and a nurturing environment, she developed a toolkit of coping strategies to manage stress and channel her emotions in healthier ways.

"Food for Flow" and Heart Rate Variability-Based Nutrition

The concept of "Food for Flow" and heart rate variability (HRV)-based nutrition is an emerging approach in the field of sports nutrition that focuses on optimizing an athlete's physiological state and performance by tailoring their diet to their unique HRV patterns.

HRV is a measure of the variation in time between consecutive heartbeats, which reflects the body's autonomic nervous system function and adaptability to stress. Studies have shown that higher HRV is associated with better health, resilience, and performance, while lower HRV may indicate overtraining, fatigue, or impaired recovery. By tracking an athlete's HRV using wearable devices or smartphone apps, nutritionists can identify patterns and make personalized recommendations to support optimal autonomic balance and performance (Hoolihan, 2022).

Some key principles of HRV-based nutrition include

- **Nutrient timing:** Consuming specific nutrients at strategic times based on HRV patterns. For example, if an athlete's HRV is low in the morning, indicating a sympathetic dominant state, they may benefit from a higher-fat, lower-carbohydrate breakfast to stabilize blood sugar and support recovery. Conversely, if HRV is high before a workout, a higher-carbohydrate meal or snack may be recommended to fuel performance.

- **Macronutrient balance:** Adjusting the ratios of carbohydrates, proteins, and fats based on individual HRV responses. Some athletes may find that a higher-carbohydrate diet supports better HRV and performance, while others may thrive on a higher-fat, lower-carbohydrate approach. Experimentation and tracking are key to finding the optimal balance for each individual.

- **Food quality:** Emphasizing whole, minimally processed foods that support gut health, reduce inflammation, and promote stable blood sugar levels. This may include plenty of colorful fruits and vegetables, high-quality proteins, healthy fats, and fermented foods.

- **Stress management:** Incorporating stress-reducing practices like mindful eating, deep breathing, and relaxation techniques to support healthy HRV and overall well-being.

Still, it is important to note that HRV-based nutrition is still an emerging field, and more research is needed to fully understand its potential applications and limitations. Athletes and nutritionists should use HRV monitoring as one tool in a comprehensive approach to performance optimization, alongside other proven strategies like proper training periodization, sleep hygiene, and stress management.

Periodization and Training Cycles

Periodization, pioneered by Tudor Bompa, structures an athlete's training into distinct phases with specific goals (Bompa & Haff, 2009). It involves manipulating volume, intensity, and specificity over time. The aim is to guide the athlete's development to peak at the right moments while minimizing injury risk, burnout, and stagnation.

Structuring Training to Peak at the Right Times

Effective periodization aims to achieve "peaking"—reaching optimal performance readiness at a specific point in time, usually coinciding with a major competition or event. To accomplish this, the training year is divided into several main phases, each building upon the previous phase's adaptations.

The first phase, known as the "preparatory" or "base" phase, focuses on building a solid foundation of general physical preparedness. This phase involves a high volume of low-to-moderate intensity work, emphasizing aerobic conditioning, muscular endurance, and basic movement skills. For example, a sprinter might focus on longer, slower runs, bodyweight circuits, and technique drills to develop a strong conditioning and movement efficiency base.

As the competitive season approaches, training enters the "specific" or "precompetitive" phase, narrowing the focus to more sport-specific skills and qualities. Training volume may decrease slightly, while intensity increases. Our sprinter might incorporate more explosive plyometric drills, shorter, faster interval sessions, and specific technique work to refine skills and prepare for competition demands.

Finally, as the main competition nears, the athlete enters the "peaking" or "tapering" phase, significantly reducing training volume while maintaining high intensity. This allows for maximal recovery and freshness leading into the event while providing enough stimulus to maintain peak fitness. Our sprinter's workouts might consist of short, snappy sprints, low-volume plyometrics, and ample rest and recovery to ensure peak performance on race day.

Periodization is crucial for targeting peak performance times, planning preseason conditioning and skill development periods, increasing physical intensity and competition, and allowing time for integration, restoration, and recovery. The annual schedule should incorporate target goals, preseason, off-season, vacations, family events, work obligations, build periods, taper periods, and intensity training, enabling the body to assimilate efforts. Frequency, volume, duration of efforts, consistency, and recovery periods with fun cross-training activities are all essential considerations. Optimizing and sustaining the benefits from previous cycles and/or injuries is also vital. Dividing the 12-month calendar into weeks and days makes each goal achievable.

Cross-Training for Balanced Development

Cross-training involves incorporating activities outside an athlete's primary sport or discipline to promote balanced physical development, prevent overuse injuries, and maintain psychological freshness. For example, a distance runner might benefit from regular cycling or swimming sessions to maintain cardiovascular fitness while reducing joint impact stress. A gymnast might use yoga or Pilates to improve flexibility, body control, and core stability, enhancing performance on the mat or apparatus.

Effective cross-training should target areas of weakness or imbalance while providing a mental break from the monotony of sport-specific training. It offers an opportunity to develop new skills, challenge the body in novel ways, and reignite the joy and passion for movement that can sometimes be lost in the grind of competitive preparation. For instance, a swimmer with limited shoulder flexibility might incorporate regular yoga sessions to improve range of motion and reduce the risk of overuse injuries.

One particularly effective strategy is implementing "contrast" training blocks, dedicating a focused period (usually 2–4 weeks) to a complementary discipline before returning to sport-specific training. These training blocks allow athletes to concentrate on developing specific aspects of their fitness or performance. For instance, a mixed martial arts)fighter might spend a training block focusing on pure strength development in the gym, using compound lifts and accessory work to build raw power and muscle mass. They might then transition to a block of high-volume kettlebell conditioning to improve work capacity and endurance before returning to sparring and technical skill work leading up to a fight.

Alternating through these contrasting stimuli mitigates stagnation, sustains athlete engagement, and cultivates a more well-rounded, resilient athlete. The key is to select activities that complement the primary sport's demands, address individual weaknesses, and provide a fun, engaging challenge.

Conditioning or training balances sport-specific skills of strength, speed, endurance, flexibility, and core strength. Ideally, athletes should develop effective routines for pre-, during-, and post-activities with the guidance of a coach. Additionally, travel and altitude can be significant stressors on the body, making it important to acclimate to altitude as mountaineers do, climbing high and sleeping low for recovery and allowing the body to adjust.

For example, as a mountaineer preparing for a steep climb, I initially trained by loading my backpack with weights. However, I've discovered a more efficient and enjoyable approach: using water as a weight in a sled. I fill containers with water and place them in the sled. Then, wearing snowshoes or crampons, I trudge uphill while pulling the loaded sled behind me, simulating the heavy loads I'll need to carry during my actual climb. When I reach the top of the training hill, I pour out the water, which makes the sled lighter for the descent. This approach not only adds a fun element to my training process but also provides a more sport-specific conditioning experience. The ski down is also more enjoyable with the lighter load.

Rest and Recovery

In the relentless pursuit of athletic excellence, it's easy to get caught up in the "more is better" mindset—more hours in the gym, more miles on the track, more reps, more sets, more pain, more gain. However, as any seasoned athlete or coach can attest, the real magic happens not just in the crucible of intense training but in the quiet, restorative spaces between those bouts of effort. It's in those crucial periods of rest and recovery that the body and mind truly adapt, grow, and come back stronger than before.

The Body's Recovery Systems

The immune system and relaxation response play crucial roles in an athlete's recovery process.

Intense physical activity can temporarily suppress the immune system, increasing the risk of illness and injury. To maintain a robust immune system, athletes should prioritize sleep, which helps regulate the immune response, promote tissue repair, and reduce inflammation. Consuming a variety of colorful fruits and vegetables rich in vitamins, minerals, and antioxidants, along with adequate protein intake and healthy fats like omega-3s, also supports immune function.

The relaxation response, characterized by decreased heart rate, blood pressure, and muscle tension, counters the negative effects of the fight-or-flight response activated during stress. Engaging in stress-reducing activities like deep breathing exercises, meditation, yoga, spending time in nature, and massage therapy can help activate the relaxation response and promote overall health and well-being.

Rest and Recovery Strategies for Peak Performance

To optimize recovery and performance, athletes should incorporate a range of strategies into their training regimen.

1. Balancing Training Intensity With Recovery

Reaching a true peak demands more than merely grinding out hard workouts. It's a delicate balance of pushing the body to adapt and grow while allowing sufficient recovery and regeneration time. Overload without adequate recovery leads to burnout, injury, and stagnation.

This is where the art and science of coaching shine. A skilled coach must read an athlete's individual response to training, considering factors like age, training history, lifestyle stressors, and subjective feedback. Diligently tracking markers like resting heart rate, sleep quality, mood, and workout performance enables real-time adjustments to the training plan, optimizing the stress and recovery balance.

In addition to subjective measures, coaches, and athletes can leverage objective tools like HRV monitoring to gauge recovery status. As mentioned earlier, HRV reflects the body's autonomic nervous system function and adaptability to stress. By tracking HRV daily, athletes can gain valuable insights into their readiness to train and make informed decisions about when to push harder or pull back.

If an athlete's HRV drops significantly below their baseline, it may indicate the need for additional recovery, such as an extra rest day or a reduced training load. Coaches can use this information to adjust training plans in real time, helping athletes avoid overtraining and maintain optimal performance.

Another critical aspect of managing intensity and recovery is utilizing "deloading" phases. A deload is a planned period of reduced training volume and/or intensity, usually lasting a week or two, allowing for a concentrated block of physical and mental recovery. Deloads are typically incorporated every 4–8 weeks, tailored to the athlete's individual needs.

During a deload, training volume is reduced by 30%–50% while maintaining relatively high intensity to preserve fitness. For example, a powerlifter's training might decrease from 4 days per week to 2 while still working up to heavy singles or doubles on main lifts. The goal is to significantly reduce overall training stress without detraining or losing too much hard-earned fitness.

Finally, include complete rest days in the training schedule to allow for physical and mental recovery. During these days, engage in low-intensity activities like yoga, stretching, or light walking to promote relaxation and facilitate active recovery without adding undue stress to the body.

You will also need to plan recovery weeks every 4–6 weeks, depending on the intensity of your training cycle. During these weeks, significantly reduce training volume and intensity to allow for a more comprehensive recovery of the musculoskeletal, nervous, and endocrine systems.

2. Nutrition

Support recovery through a balanced diet rich in colorful fruits and vegetables, lean proteins, and healthy fats.

With the intense physical and mental demands placed on today's athletes, the strategic use of supplements can also be a valuable tool for supporting recovery and preventing overtraining syndrome.

One of the most extensively researched supplements in this realm is creatine monohydrate. Creatine is a naturally occurring compound that plays a key role in energy production, particularly during high-intensity efforts. By supplementing with creatine, athletes can boost their muscle stores of this valuable resource, leading to increased strength and power output, improved recovery between sets, and potentially even enhanced cognitive function.

Be aware that creatine supplementation requires an increased intake of water to help process it effectively. Creatine works by drawing water into the muscle cells, which can lead to a slight increase in water retention and body weight. Therefore, athletes should be mindful of staying well-hydrated when supplementing with creatine to ensure optimal performance and avoid potential side effects such as cramping or digestive issues.

Omega-3 fatty acids, typically derived from fish oil, are another staple in many athletes' supplement regimens. The potent anti-inflammatory properties of omega-3s can help counteract exercise-induced muscle damage and soreness, promoting faster recovery between training sessions. They also support cardiovascular health, brain function, and mood—all critical factors in overall athletic performance.

For athletes engaging in particularly intense or prolonged training blocks, incorporating branched-chain amino acids (BCAAs) into their routines is often recommended. BCAAs are a specific subset of essential amino acids that play a crucial role in muscle protein synthesis and can help reduce muscle breakdown during exercise. By sipping on a BCAA drink during lengthy training sessions or competitions, athletes may be able to stave off fatigue, reduce post-exercise soreness, and speed up recovery times.

An often-overlooked area of supplementation for athletes is gut health support. The gut microbiome—the trillions of bacteria that inhabit our digestive tract—plays a surprisingly significant role in everything from nutrient absorption to immune function to mental well-being. By incorporating probiotic-rich foods like yogurt, kefir, kimchi, and sauerkraut, or taking a high-quality probiotic supplement daily, athletes can help maintain thriving gut flora and support overall health and resilience.

It is important to stress the importance of choosing supplements wisely and working closely with a qualified healthcare professional to develop a personalized plan. While supplements can be incredibly useful tools, they are just that—tools in a much larger toolbox of nutrition, hydration, sleep, stress management, and smart training practices.

3. Sleep Well and Recover Right

Sleep allows the body and mind to repair, recharge, and come back stronger. It should be treated as a nonnegotiable component of your training regimen, with a target of 7–9 hours of quality sleep each night.

However, for some athletes, even 10 hours of quality sleep may be necessary to optimize recovery and preparedness for the next day's flow experience.

Create a sleep sanctuary by keeping your bedroom cool, dark, and quiet. Stick to a consistent sleep-wake schedule, even on weekends. In the evening hours, avoid stimulating activities and blue light exposure from screens, as this can disrupt your circadian rhythms and melatonin production. Instead, wind down with relaxing practices like breath work, gentle yoga, or meditation to signal your mind and body to prepare for rest.

There are a myriad of devices and apps available to support individual needs, from sleep-tracking apps like Sleep Cycle and SleepScore to breathing exercises and relaxing sounds for bedtime routines, such as Calm and Headspace.

Among them, the Oura ring is a key tool in my personal coaching and recovery journey. This app provides valuable insights into my sleep stages, duration, recovery status, and overall HRV readiness each morning. This data helps confirm my subjective feelings and guides my daily planning.

For example, if my Oura ring indicates that I had a poor night's sleep with limited deep and REM sleep, I know that I may need to adjust my training plan for the day to allow for more recovery. On the other hand, if my Oura ring shows that I had a restorative night's sleep with ample time spent in deep and REM stages, I feel more confident pushing myself harder in my training sessions.

However, I've also learned that while these tools can be incredibly helpful, they should be used to support a well-rounded approach to recovery and self-care. It's easy to fall into the trap of overworking and not allocating sufficient time for proper rest and relaxation, even on days off. Creating a realistic plan that balances work, fun, and recovery is essential, rather than simply filling every moment with activity. Using tools like the Oura ring in conjunction with a mindful, balanced approach to training and life has allowed me to optimize my sleep, recovery, and overall well-being.

If you struggle with sleep quality or consistency, tracking your patterns can reveal issues like irregular bedtimes, stress, or blue light disruptions. Make adjustments accordingly to ensure restorative sleep filled with renewing deep, REM, and light stages. This prepares your mind–body to operate in optimal flow and achieve peak performance day after day.

Cultivating Embodied Awareness

While the previous sections have focused on the physical aspects of aligning the body for peak performance, strong optimization further involves the harmonious integration of mind and body. Embodied conditioning is a powerful approach to increase this integration, allowing athletes to develop a deep, intuitive connection between their mental and physical processes. In the following subsections, we'll explore the key components of embodied conditioning, including tuning into physical sensations, unlocking muscle memory and intuitive responses, balancing strength, flexibility, and agility, and developing stability, mobility, and core strength.

Tuning Into Physical Sensations

At the heart of embodied cognition and somatic awareness lies the critical skill of tuning into our physical sensations. This practice involves developing a heightened sensitivity to the subtle cues, impulses, and feelings that arise within our bodies from moment to moment, and learning to interpret and respond to this valuable information in ways that promote health, well-being, and optimal functioning.

For many of us, the constant demands and distractions of modern life have left us disconnected from our bodily experiences, operating primarily from the neck up as we see the world through the lens of our thoughts and mental abstractions. We may go through our days barely noticing the signals our bodies are sending us, whether it's the tight knot of tension in our shoulders, the fluttering of anxiety in our chests, or the warm glow of contentment that arises when we're engaged in a meaningful activity.

However, as the pioneering work of researchers like Antonio Damasio and Bud Craig has shown, our physical sensations play a vital role in shaping our emotions, decision-making processes, and overall sense of mind–body (Damasio, 1994; Craig, 2009). If we can tune into these sensations with greater awareness and clarity, we'll open up a powerful channel for new understanding, emotional regulation, and intuitive wisdom.

One of the foundational practices for cultivating somatic attunement is body scan meditation, which involves systematically directing my attention through the various regions of my body, noticing any sensations, tensions, or areas of ease that I encounter along the way.

An easy way I like to practice this is to do a body scan right before falling asleep. As I lie in bed, ready for slumber, I start by bringing my awareness to my toes. I slowly breathe into that area, tuning into the physical sensations present there. Then I move my focus up to my feet, calves, knees, and so on—systematically working my way up my body with gentle curiosity. I see how far I can journey through my bodily landscape before drifting off into restful sleep.

This full-body awareness practice helps me refine my nuanced experience of physical sensation. It can also provide a valuable release of chronic muscle tension and holding patterns as I bring a soft, accepting attention to each region of my body in turn.

Another aspect of tuning into physical sensations is learning to recognize and interpret the language of our autonomic nervous system, which communicates with us through a range of visceral cues and responses. For example, the sensation of a racing heart, sweaty palms, and a tightening in our gut may be our body's way of signaling that we're in a state of high arousal or anxiety.

On those nights, I may need to breathe longer into these areas of tension and consciously release the pent-up energy through extended exhales. In contrast, feelings of warmth, relaxation, and expansiveness may indicate that my body is in a more parasympathetic state of rest and restoration, where I can allow myself to fully embrace the tranquility through deep, soothing breaths.

By attuning to these visceral messages from my autonomic nervous system and responding with techniques like focused breathing, I'm able to modulate my physiological state in a more optimal direction—downregulating excessive arousal when needed, or accentuating the relaxation response when conditions are ripe. This mind–body dialogue allows me to navigate my innate rhythms with greater awareness and mastery.

At a deeper level, tuning into our physical sensations can also help us tap into the vast reservoir of embodied knowledge and intuition that lies beyond the reach of our conscious minds. Our bodies are constantly processing a wealth of information about our environment, our relationships, and our own inner wisdom, and this information is often communicated to us through subtle feelings, hunches, and gut reactions.

Once we can trust and attune to these somatic signals, we can access a powerful source of guidance and wisdom that can inform our choices, enrich our lives, and help us handle the complexities of the human experience with greater ease and grace. This might involve regular practices of mindful movement, such as yoga, tai chi, or qigong, which can help us refine our sensitivity to the language of our bodies and develop a more harmonious and integrated enactive embodiment.

After a strenuous workout, I relish lying on the floor and stretching out while paying close attention to any intuitive thoughts or gut feelings that arise. This practice of embodied listening proves invaluable when I'm paragliding. Making those intuitive calls in the air about which thermal to turn into or adjusting my trajectory draws from the same somatic intelligence. Trusting my instincts is crucial not only for optimizing my flight path but also for avoiding the risk of landing out before reaching my designated goal.

During long, persistent flights tagging various waypoints from the sky, not second-guessing my gut instinct becomes essential for success and ensuring that I reach my target. Paragliding demands an ongoing dance of challenging yet fun experiences—handling that embodied-flow experience while trusting the physical intuitions that allow me to thrive and complete the task as planned or adapt the route to the ever-changing sun, shade, and cloud formations.

Unlocking Muscle Memory and Intuitive Responses

In the realm of athletic performance, the ability to execute complex skills and techniques with fluid, unconscious ease is often referred to as "muscle memory." This concept has been extensively studied by researchers like Dr. Richard A. Schmidt (2003), a leading authority on motor learning and control.

According to Schmidt's (2003) "schema theory," our brains create generalized motor programs or "schemas" that govern specific classes of movements, such as throwing a ball or swinging a golf club. These schemas are based on a set of rules or parameters that define the essential features of the movement, such as the relative timing and force of the muscle contractions involved.

Through repetitive practice, these schemas become increasingly refined and automated, allowing us to execute the movements with greater precision and consistency. However, Schmidt emphasized that the key to developing robust, adaptable schemas is not just mindless repetition, but "variable practice"—that is, practicing the skill under a variety of different conditions and contexts.

For example, a basketball player might practice shooting from different distances, angles, and positions on the court, or with varying degrees of defensive pressure. They can develop a more flexible, resilient set of motor programs that can be readily adapted to the demands of real-game situations by exposing themselves to a wide range of challenges and variations.

Unlocking muscle memory and intuitive responses is learning to trust in the body's innate intelligence and letting go of conscious control while unlocking muscle memory and intuitive responses as well. Considering this, I invite you to examine the work of Dr. Gabriele Wulf (2013), a leading researcher in the field of attentional focus and motor learning.

Wulf's research on attentional focus illuminates the organizing potential of the body in achieving optimal performance. When athletes direct their attention externally to the intended movement effect, rather than internally to the mechanics of their own body, they tap into embodied flow characterized by greater accuracy, fluidity, and ease.

This phenomenon points to the inherent wisdom of the mind–body system when allowed to operate without interference from conscious control. By shifting awareness away from the internal minutiae of movement and trusting in the body's natural intelligence, athletes can access a heightened state of coordination and embodied flow.

However, it's important to recognize that this organizing potential is not separate from the conscious mind, but rather a reflection of the profound integration and attunement of mind–body. Embodied flow emerges when the two are working in seamless harmony, with the conscious mind providing a clear intention and then stepping back to allow the body to execute with its full wisdom and power.

This synergy of mental clarity and physical intuition lies at the heart of peak performance. It enables athletes to become entirely consumed by the unfolding moment, free from the doubts and distractions of the thinking mind. In this way of being, with unified consciousness and action, the athlete becomes a conduit for the full expression of their embodied potential.

To cultivate this level of mind–body attunement, athletes can complement external focus techniques with practices that deepen their felt sense of embodied awareness. Mindfulness meditation, somatic exploration, and breath-centered movement can all help to refine one's sensitivity to the subtle cues and impulses arising from within.

Over time, this inner attunement enables athletes to develop an instinctive trust in their body's signals and a profound respect for its innate intelligence. They discover that peak performance is not about imposing the mind's will upon the body, but about learning to listen to and align with its natural rhythms and embodying flow.

Another valuable tool is to incorporate "external cueing" into our practice routines. This might involve using visual markers or targets to guide our movements or focusing on the sound or feel of the equipment we're using (such as the crisp snap of a well-struck golf ball or the smooth, effortless glide of a ski on fresh powder).

Advances in video analysis software have opened up exciting new possibilities for external cueing and skill refinement, especially during periods when athletes are unable to practice their sport in real-world conditions. For example, golfers can now use sophisticated programs that combine motion capture technology with virtual reality simulations to analyze and perfect their swing mechanics.

By seeing a detailed breakdown of their movement patterns and ball flight characteristics, athletes can identify subtle flaws or inconsistencies that might be holding them back. They can then experiment with different adjustments and receive immediate feedback on the impact of those changes, whether it's reducing a slice, increasing distance, or dialing in their accuracy.

This kind of virtual practice can be a game-changer during the off-season, allowing athletes to continue refining their skills and ingraining optimal movement patterns even when they don't have access to a course or real-world training facilities. And through the combination of this technology and the principles of external cueing—focusing on the desired outcome rather than the internal mechanics of the movement—athletes can accelerate their progress and develop a greater sense of embodied flow.

Of course, these virtual tools are not a replacement for real-world practice and competition, but rather a complementary training aid. The ultimate goal is to cultivate a fluid, intuitive sense of connection between the athlete's intention, their body's movement, and the equipment or environment they are interacting with.

By training this integrated awareness and action, whether through virtual simulations or real-world drills, athletes can develop the kind of adaptable, resilient skills that will serve them in the heat of competition. They can learn to trust their body's intelligence and let go of conscious control, allowing their movements to flow with effortless grace and precision.

Balancing Strength, Flexibility, and Agility

When it comes to physical conditioning, there is often a tendency to focus on one particular aspect of fitness at the expense of others. However, true functional fitness requires a balanced and integrative approach that addresses all the key components of physical readiness: strength, flexibility, agility, balance, and coordination.

Strength refers to the ability to generate force and power, which is essential for explosive movements and resistance against external loads. Flexibility, on the other hand, is the capacity to move joints through a full range of motion, allowing for fluid and efficient movement patterns. Agility is the ability to change direction and react quickly to dynamic situations, which is crucial for sports that require rapid transitions and responsiveness.

Balancing these three components is essential for optimal performance and injury prevention. An athlete who focuses solely on strength training may develop powerful muscles but lack the flexibility and agility needed for smooth, coordinated movements. Conversely, an athlete who prioritizes flexibility and agility without adequate strength may be more susceptible to injuries and limited in their power output.

Take cycling, for example. The repetitive, forward-leaning position and pedaling motion can lead to adaptations like rounded shoulders, tight hip flexors, and weak core muscles over time. To counteract these sport-specific imbalances and maintain optimal function, cyclists need to cross-train in a way that specifically targets their positional blind spots and movement limitations, incorporating exercises that promote spinal mobility, hip flexibility, and core stability.

The principle of targeted cross-training applies to all athletes. The best approach is tailored to individual needs and goals, based on a careful assessment of movement patterns, physical limitations, and performance aspirations. The Functional Movement Screen (FMS), created by Dr. Gray Cook (2010), is designed to identify weak links and compensatory patterns, providing a roadmap for targeted corrective exercise and training. By assessing fundamental movement patterns, the

FMS helps pinpoint areas of restriction, weakness, or dysfunction that may be limiting performance or setting the stage for injury.

Once these imbalances have been identified, the goal is to develop a comprehensive training program that addresses the specific needs and deficits of the individual, using a combination of targeted strength work, flexibility and mobility drills, and neuromuscular control and coordination training. The key is to maintain a broad, inclusive perspective that recognizes the interdependence of all the various components of functional fitness, laying the groundwork for optimal performance and resilience in any activity or pursuit.

This integrative approach is echoed by other leading voices in the field, such as Dr. Kelly Starrett (2015), who emphasizes the importance of regularly assessing and refining basic movement patterns using tools like foam rolling, lacrosse balls, and resistance bands to address areas of tension, restriction, and dysfunction. By taking a proactive and preventative approach, we can optimize short-term performance and lay the foundation for lifelong health and vitality.

Circling back to Jessie Diggins's journey, her comprehensive physical preparation involved innovative biomechanical assessments at the U.S. Ski & Snowboard's Center of Excellence (2023). This facility utilizes advanced technologies to identify imbalances or inefficiencies in her movement patterns.

Based on these insights, she followed specialized strength and mobility programs designed to refine her technique and minimize the risk of injury. Her yearly training and competition schedule was carefully planned to allow for targeted preparation and peak performance at key events like the World Cup and Tour de Ski. This strategic approach helped her manage workloads effectively and avoid overtraining or burnout.

And surrounding her was an incredible support system—from coaches like Matt Whitcomb providing technical mastery, to teammates fostering a nurturing culture, to family anchoring her emotionally (Theyerl, 2024; Shinn, 2021). Diggins cultivated a 360-degree web of support, empowerment, and accountability.

This team helped her deal with the intense physical and mental demands. Her coaches meticulously mapped out her racing schedule and ramp-up plan, while her support circle provided encouragement and stability.

Diggins also benefited from the expertise of a top-notch waxing tech team. In cross-country skiing, optimizing ski waxing and base preparations for specific snow conditions is absolutely critical for maximizing glide and traction. Diggins worked closely with a dedicated group of wax technicians who analyzed weather data, tested numerous wax compounds, and dialed in her skis to absolute perfection before every race. Their behind-the-scenes efforts to gain every possible fraction of a second through meticulous waxing were indispensable in Diggins's ability to reach the sport's pinnacle.

Still, her greatest asset was the remarkable mental fortitude required to push past perceived limits and enter what she calls the "pain cave" during competitions. Jessie Diggins describes the "pain cave" as that transcendent state where endurance athletes must confront unfathomable physical suffering. In that crucible space, every fiber of her being screamed for mercy as searing lactic acid flooded her muscles, her vision blurred, and her hearing dulled.

Yet, Diggins learned to befriend the anguish rather than resist it, maintaining an intense, unwavering focus to push far beyond where the true embodied flow thought possible. Her ability to dwell in and even harness the "pain cave" became a defining hallmark of her resilience, exemplifying how like icons such as Usain Bolt, she refused to let perceived limits define her potential for transcendent feats.

Diggins's training is designed to simulate and prepare her for these intense conditions. Her workouts often involve pushing her body to the edge of its capabilities. For example, during training sessions, she might perform repeated climbs up steep inclines, mimicking the arduous effort required in her races. Diggins also conditioned her physiology to thrive across the extreme cold, altitude, and other environmental stressors through cold exposure training inspired by "Iceman" Wim Hof and breath work to up-regulate her parasympathetic response.

When it comes to mental strategies, mindfulness techniques and cognitive behavioral approaches allow her to maintain focus and composure under extreme stress. By training her mind to remain calm and determined, she can push through the pain and maintain her performance. Rather than resisting the pain, Diggins has learned to embrace it. She sees the "pain cave" as a necessary part of her journey to greatness, a place where she can test her limits and discover new levels of resilience, as well as surprising even her new levels of embodied peak performance flow (International Olympic Committee, n.d.).

Stability, Mobility, and Core Strength

Stability, mobility, and core strength form the foundation upon which all other aspects of performance and resilience rest. They prove essential for preventing injuries, moving efficiently, and promoting overall well-being.

While closely related to strength, flexibility, and agility, they are distinct concepts that focus on the foundational elements of efficient, injury-resistant movement.

Stability

Stability refers to the ability to maintain balance, alignment, and control in a given position or movement, even when faced with external forces or disturbances. This critical skill allows athletes and fitness enthusiasts to generate and transfer force efficiently, maintain proper form and technique, and minimize the risk of injuries. For cross-country skiers and paragliders, stability is crucial for achieving smooth and efficient movement.

In cross-country skiing, an engaged core and balanced body position enable the skier to transfer power effectively from the legs to the poles, maintaining a consistent glide and rhythm. Similarly, in paragliding, stability in the harness allows the pilot to maintain control and make precise inputs, even in turbulent conditions. By developing a strong foundation of stability, athletes in these sports can optimize their performance and enjoy a more fluid, effortless experience.

A vital component of stability, proprioception enables the body to sense and respond to its own position and movement in space. A complex network of sensory receptors in our muscles, tendons, and joints governs this, providing feedback to the brain about our embodied movement, balance, and movement.

Dr. Vladimir Janda, a musculoskeletal rehabilitation pioneer, recommended various exercises to develop proprioceptive awareness and stability. These might include single-leg stands, balance board work, or unstable surface training using tools like BOSU balls or foam pads (Janda, 1983).

For me, I often imagine a gentle string pulling me upright through the spine, lengthening from the crown of my head. I apply this alignment cue across activities—from dressage riding to yoga to paragliding. It promotes an upright yet relaxed posture that allows my breath to move freely and my body to sense subtle cues, whether feeling the shifting weight of a horse or detecting rising air currents as I fly.

Challenging the ability to maintain equilibrium and control in unstable or unpredictable environments engages the neural network of embodied flow, refining the communication between our brain and body. As a result, these exercises enhance the overall stability and resilience of the individual, allowing them to perform with greater ease, efficiency, and adaptability in various physical pursuits.

Mobility

Closely related, mobility refers to the ability to move smoothly and efficiently through a full range of motion without undue tension, restriction, or compensation. This ability proves essential for optimal performance and overall health and longevity.

In his book *Becoming a Supple Leopard*, Dr. Kelly Starrett emphasizes that many people have developed chronic patterns of stiffness, tightness, and dysfunction due to sedentary lifestyles, poor posture, and repetitive stress (Starrett & Cordoza, 2013). These restrictions can limit the ability to move freely and efficiently, setting the stage for pain, injuries, and suboptimal performance.

Starrett recommends a comprehensive mobility training approach. This includes targeted stretching, myofascial release techniques like foam rolling and lacrosse ball work, and dynamic, full-range-of-motion exercises that challenge the ability to move smoothly and fluidly. Through a series of simple drills and cues, like "screwing your feet into the floor" or "bracing your abdomen as if you're about to take a punch," Starrett teaches people how to find and maintain that neutral alignment in any position or movement (Starrett, 2013).

The results are often remarkable—athletes who have struggled with chronic back pain suddenly find themselves moving with ease and fluidity, while others see dramatic improvements in their strength and power output.

Systematically identifying and addressing areas of restriction and dysfunction, while regularly exposing our bodies to a wide range of movement challenges, gradually restores natural mobility and freedom of movement. It's crucial to choose training methods that you enjoy and that align with your personal goals of flow activation.

By focusing on the process and selecting activities that bring you joy and fulfillment, you'll be more likely to stay motivated and committed to your mobility practice.

Remember, the key is to strike a balance between challenging yourself and listening to your body so that you can make consistent progress while avoiding burnout or injury.

Core Strength

No discussion proves complete without addressing the crucial role of core strength. Dr. Stuart McGill, a leading expert on spine biomechanics and back pain, emphasizes that the core represents more than just isolated muscles. Instead, it constitutes a complex and integrated system vital to almost every aspect of human movement and performance (McGill, 2015).

As McGill defines it, the core includes not just the superficial abdominal muscles like the rectus abdominis (six-pack), but also the deeper stabilizing muscles of the spine, pelvis, and trunk, such as the transverse abdominis, multifidus, and pelvic floor. These muscles work together to provide a stable foundation for movement, transfer force efficiently between the upper and lower body, and protect the spine from injury and stress.

McGill recommends exercises that challenge the ability to maintain spinal alignment and control under load to develop true core strength and stability. These might include variations of the plank, bird dog, side bridge, and more dynamic, functional movements like the Turkish get-up or Pallof press.

For athletes like skate skiers and paragliders, these exercises can be particularly valuable.

In skate skiing, a strong core is essential for maintaining an efficient double pole technique, which involves a powerful abdominal crunch motion to generate propulsive force.

Similarly, in paragliding, a stable core helps maintain balanced pressure control while maneuvering the glider, enabling the pilot to efficiently reach the top of a thermal before it dissipates.

When incorporating these targeted core exercises into their training regimen, athletes in these disciplines can develop the specific strength and stability needed to optimize their performance and minimize the risk of injury.

The key, as McGill emphasizes, lies in focusing not on isolated strength or endurance, but on the quality and efficiency of the movement itself. Engaging the core musculature in a coordinated and synergistic way, while maintaining proper alignment and breathing mechanics, such as in weekly weight lifting routines, develops a strong, resilient, and adaptable core capable of withstanding even the most challenging activities and movements.

I have poured over these closing words, striving to do justice to the reverence I feel for Jessie's journey, for the strength, the passion, and the sheer determination underlying her every forward step.

Diggins's story, which we've explored throughout this chapter, is one of triumph over adversity. From her struggles with bulimia to her historic Olympic gold medal, Diggins proves that with courage and perseverance, one can overcome immense challenges and reach unprecedented heights.

That said, Diggins's approach to peak performance extends far beyond nutrition alone. She has developed a holistic way of being that encompasses every aspect of her life, from her daily rituals and training routines to her recovery strategies and mind–body health practices.

Taking cues from her multifaceted approach, the next chapter will explore the power of rituals, routines, and recovery practices in creating the conditions for peak performance and sustained well-being. Just as Diggins's morning routines set the tone for her day, her diverse cross-training regimen builds resilience and prevents burnout, and her commitment to nurturing her overall well-being forms the bedrock of her extraordinary achievements, we'll examine how elite performers across various fields harness similar practices to reach their full potential.

However, as we embark on this exploration, let us not lose sight of the true North Star guiding our journey—Diggins's inspiring story. Let it remind each of us of our own inherent ability to embody flow and craft lives of meaning, resilience, and profound contribution. Let us remember that, no matter how daunting the challenges may seem, we all have the power within us to rise above, heal, grow, and achieve the seemingly impossible. And through her example, we see that true peak performance is not just about pushing harder, but about nurturing a life of balance, joy, and purpose.

The journey will be bumpy and full of surprises—but it will be exquisitely, uniquely ours. And it will be worth every leap of faith along the way.

So, here's to the brave ones, the trailblazers, the ones who dare to dream big and fight fiercely for their vision; enacting a world of unknown possibility and mind–body potential. May we all find the courage to follow in their footsteps, to trust in the wisdom of our own hearts, and to never, ever give up on the magic that lies waiting just beyond our comfort zones.

Chapter 4:

The Three Rs Toward Embodying Flow—Rituals, Routines, and Recovery

At first glance, rituals, routines, and recovery might seem mundane, even trivial. However, the deliberate implementation of these practices allows the seeds of greatness to take root and flourish. Rituals, routines, and recovery play a crucial role in creating the optimal conditions for what experts call "micro-flow experiences"—brief moments of flow that we can encounter in everyday activities. These micro-flow experiences provide a taste of the benefits associated with flow, such as heightened focus, improved performance, and increased well-being.

Rituals, routines, and recovery contribute to the emergence of micro-flow experiences by acting as a bridge between our conscious intentions and our subconscious mind, strengthening the mind–body connection. They establish a consistent and familiar pattern of behavior, reducing cognitive load and decision fatigue, and freeing up our attentional resources to focus on the task at hand. The repetition of specific behaviors and actions through rituals, routines, and recovery also helps to create strong neural pathways in the brain, conditioning our mind–bodies to more readily access heightened awareness, focus, and performance.

Pre-Activity Rituals and Routines

Pre-activity rituals and routines hold a pivotal role: shepherding individuals from life's incessant demands and distractions into focused, flow-primed experiences.

Shedding cognitive load and conquering decision fatigue stands as a central way pre-activity rituals hit their mark. But their impact transcends the mental realm—they regulate our physiological arousal, priming bodies for optimized performance. Neuroscientist Dr. Wendy Suzuki's studies at New York University demonstrate how even short exercise bouts bolster cognitive abilities and drive neurotrophic factor production, supporting brain cell flourishing. Blending physical warm-ups and stretching into pre-activity rituals unlocks these advantages, unifying mind and body harmoniously (Suzuki, 2023).

However, the power of pre-activity rituals is not just about the physical. Visualization and meditation techniques, for example, have been shown to activate many of the same neural pathways as actual experience, creating what Dr. Richard Restak (2009), a renowned neuroscientist and author, calls "a mental rehearsal of future actions." When we mentally rehearse the challenges we will face and the way we will overcome them, we can build confidence, reduce anxiety, and prime ourselves for success.

Other pre-activity rituals, like listening to specific music or reciting mantras, can also have a meaningful impact on our mental and emotional states. Research by Dr. Costas Karageorghis, a leading expert on the psychology of music in sport and exercise, has shown that carefully selected music can enhance mood, reduce perceived exertion, and even synchronize brain waves to promote embodied flow (Karageorghis, 2017). Similarly, mantras and affirmations can help to focus the mind, reframe negative thoughts, and cultivate a sense of efficacy and resilience.

Consider the case of legendary basketball coach Phil Jackson, who led the Chicago Bulls and Los Angeles Lakers to a combined 11 NBA championships. Jackson was an expert at using rituals and routines to help his players access flow states both on and off the court, leveraging the power of the mind–body connection. He introduced practices like mindfulness meditation, visualization, and yoga to help his teams develop greater mind–body resilience, create a shared sense of purpose, and unlock their full potential as individuals and as a collective.

One of Jackson's most efficient techniques was the use of pre-game routines to help his players transition from the chaos and distractions of everyday life into a state of focused readiness. He encouraged each player to develop their own personalized routine—a series of small, meaningful actions that would signal to their mind–body that it was time to perform (Jackson & Delehanty, 2013).

For some players, this might involve listening to a specific playlist or reciting a mantra. For others, it might mean spending a few minutes in quiet reflection or visualizing themselves executing key plays with precision and grace. The specifics mattered less than the intention behind them—to create a sacred space, a cocoon of concentration and clarity, amid the noise and turbulence of high-stakes competition.

Of course, pre-activity rituals are just one side of the equation. Equally important are the post-activity recovery practices that help us to process, integrate, and grow from our experiences. As psychologist Dr. Ron Siegel (2010) notes, "The power is not just in the experience itself, but in the recovery and reflection that follows."

Post-Activity Recovery Practices

Post-activity recovery practices have several essential functions.

First and foremost, they help to facilitate physical and mental recovery from the demands of intense performance. By engaging in practices like stretching, foam rolling, and massages, we can reduce muscle tension, promote blood flow, and prevent injury. At the same time, mindfulness and relaxation techniques can help to calm the nervous system, reduce stress, and promote a sense of balance and well-being.

Apart from physical restoration, post-activity recovery practices also provide an opportunity for reflection, learning, and growth. When taking time to review and analyze our performance, we can identify areas for improvement, celebrate our successes, and foster a growth mindset that sees challenges as opportunities for development.

This process of reflection and integration is essential for long-term success and well-being. As Dr. Alia Crum (2020), a psychologist at Stanford University, has shown in her research, the way we interpret and make meaning from our experiences can have a profound impact on our physiology, motivation, and performance over time. As such, if you engage in post-activity practices that promote a sense of coherence, compassion, and learning, you can develop the resilience and adaptability needed to thrive in the face of adversity.

So, what might these post-activity recovery practices look like in action? One powerful example comes from the world of elite sports, where many athletes engage in a practice known as "cool-down journaling." Immediately after a game or competition, athletes will take a few minutes to jot down their thoughts, feelings, and observations about their performance. They might reflect on what went well, what could have been better, what they learned from the experience, and what they would do differently or like to try next time.

This simple practice not only helps athletes process and integrate their experiences but also provides valuable data points that can inform future training and preparation. Through the identification of patterns over time, athletes and their coaches gain the ability to pinpoint specific areas for focused improvement and formulate more potent strategies for achieving success.

As a paragliding enthusiast, I've found this technique to be incredibly valuable in my own practice. I use this in my paragliding journal in addition to writing all the data in a spreadsheet to connect my perceptions to reality and reset for the next day. I start by reviewing the weather forecast, then attend the daily weather briefing where we discuss the day's conditions and plan a challenging yet achievable flight task. I also incorporate Skew-T diagram data to analyze the atmosphere's vertical profile and predict the microclimate at my flying site. This helps me determine the best strategies for using the day's energy based on the microclimate, speed needed, or adaptation plans for various routes.

Other post-activity recovery practices might include engaging in restorative activities like yoga, taking a walk in nature, or spending time in conversation with supportive friends and mentors. The key is to find practices that promote balance, connection, and renewal.

Back to Jackson's story. Apart from pre-game routines, Jackson also emphasized the importance of post-game routines—rituals that would help his players process the intense emotions of victory or defeat, learn from their experiences, and reset for the challenges ahead. This often involved gathering the team together for a brief moment of silence, a chance to collectively acknowledge the effort and sacrifice that had been given, regardless of the outcome.

By bookending the game with these purposeful practices, Jackson helped his players develop a greater sense of perspective, resilience, and adaptability. They learned to see each game not as a defining moment, but as part of a larger journey of growth and discovery, a journey that would continue long after the final whistle had blown.

The power of rituals and routines extends far beyond the world of sports, though. In fact, some of the most innovative and impactful leaders in business, the arts, and social change have used these practices to fuel their creativity, productivity, and well-being, often by tapping into the mind–body connection.

Take, for example, the daily rituals of author and activist Maya Angelou. She was a firm believer in the power of consistency and discipline, and structured her days around a series of small, intentional actions that helped her show up fully in her writing and life.

She would wake early, usually around 5:30 a.m., and begin her day with a simple breakfast and a cup of coffee. She would then retreat to a small, sparsely furnished room in her home, a sacred space that was reserved solely for her writing. She would light a candle, say a prayer of gratitude, and then sit down at her desk, ready to face the blank page.

Angelou had a specific writing routine that she followed religiously. She would write longhand on legal pads, filling page after page with her thoughts and ideas. She would write for a set period, usually about 2 hours, and then take a break to review and revise what she had written.

This disciplined approach to her craft allowed Angelou to tap into a deep wellspring of creative flow, even on days when the muse seemed to be absent. Through her dedication to the work, she built a powerful momentum that carried her through the inevitable challenges and setbacks of the writing process.

Beyond her writing practice, Angelou also made time each day for activities that nourished her mind, body, and spirit. This might include spending time in conversation with friends and loved ones.

As she balanced her intense focus and productivity with periods of rest and rejuvenation, Angelou was able to sustain her creative energy over the long haul, producing a body of work that has inspired and transformed countless lives around the world.

Creating Personalized Routines for Sustained Flow

We've learned from previous chapters that when the demands of a task are well-matched to our abilities, we can fully invest our attention and lose ourselves in the present moment. However, this balance is deeply personal and can shift over time. As such, the routines and practices that facilitate flow for one person may not work as effectively for another. Our neurological wiring, personality traits, life experiences, and current contexts all play a role in shaping the optimal conditions for us to access heightened states of consciousness and performance.

This is why I emphasize the importance of taking an individualized, exploratory approach when creating personalized routines. It's about tuning into your own rhythms, tendencies, and inner landscapes to discover what allows you to show up as your most focused, energized, and fully-expressed true nature.

There is a popularly known framework named Martin Seligman's (2011) PERMA model, which outlines five essential elements for human flourishing: Positive emotion, Engagement, Relationships, Meaning, and Accomplishment. If you understand how different routines and practices impact each of these domains for you as an individual, you can start to map out a holistic system for sustained flow and well-being.

Breath work or listening to uplifting music, for instance, may help some individuals improve positive emotions and energize themselves before a challenging task. Quiet reflection or journaling, on the other hand, may be more beneficial for others in finding their center. It's important to acknowledge that these preferences may vary from day to day, necessitating individuals to select and experiment with different techniques as their routines develop. Remaining flexible and adaptable while cultivating a profound curiosity about the psychological, emotional, and physiological states that enable you to experience engagement at its peak is paramount.

Once you identify the conditions that facilitate your personal "flow triggers," you can start experimenting with different routines and seeing how they impact your ability to access and sustain flow states over time. This is an iterative process of trying new things, reflecting on what works (or doesn't), and continuously refining your approach.

I advise you to think of it like chemistry—you are the expert alchemist, combining different "ingredients" (practices, environments, and tools) in your unique laboratory to create the elixir that unlocks your highest potential. It's a process of personal exploration, curiosity, and radical compassion.

For example, a graphic designer might find that their ideal flow routine involves exercising first thing in the morning to boost energy, followed by a healthy smoothie packed with brain-boosting nutrients. They may then sit down at their creative workstation with noise-canceling headphones playing atmospheric music to inspire flow.

A public speaker, on the other hand, may gravitate toward a pre-event routine that includes power poses to boost confidence, reciting positive affirmations, talking to themselves in the mirror, and visualizing their talk going smoothly. Talking into the mirror allows speakers to practice their delivery, make eye contact, and build self-assurance. Their post-event routine could involve journaling about areas for improvement, expressing gratitude, and doing light stretching to release tension.

The possibilities are endless, which is what makes this journey of personalized routine creation so exciting and transformative. You are undertaking the sacred work of study and actualization, unlocking the secrets to operating at your highest frequencies.

Of course, this work is not necessarily easy. We all have conditioning, doubts, and fear patterns to work through. You may encounter self-resistance or sabotaging tendencies when pushing into new routines. This is where the real growth lies—in developing the awareness, vulnerability, and grit to continue showing up and fine-tuning your personalized system.

But the rewards are worth it. Not only will you experience more frequent and sustained flow, leading to enhanced productivity, creativity, and performance, but you'll gain a profound sense of trust and purpose. You'll be living in alignment with your deepest values and essential nature.

To set you up for success, here are some practical tips:

- Start small by adding or tweaking just one routine at a time. Going slowly helps solidify new habits.

- Use technology like apps, journals, or spreadsheets to consistently track your routines and their impact on your flow states over time. This data will inform refinements.

- Stay accountable by looping in an accountability partner or coach who can support you through hurdles.

- Embrace any "slip-ups" or less-than-ideal days as valuable data points, not failures. This is all part of the learning process.

- Most importantly, celebrate each small win and new insight! You're doing a wonderfully challenging inner mind–body discovery.

Admittedly, I had wanted to end this chapter right after the practical tips section, but Alex Honnold's story just wouldn't let me. To omit his journey would be a disservice to the very essence of what we're discussing here—the incredible power of rituals and routines to unlock extraordinary human potential.

Honnold's preparation for his free solo climbs, especially his mind-blowing ascent of El Capitan, is a masterclass in developing embodied flow through methodical mental and physical training coupled with steadfast rituals.

At the core is his unwavering commitment to conditioning both mind and body for the outrageous demands of free solo climbing, where one tiny lapse in focus could be catastrophic. His training volume is insane—we're talking 40 hours per week; elite athlete levels of dedication.

On the physical side, he's got his bases covered with endurance work, strength training, and flexibility drills. But it's those dawn patrol sessions that are pure magic, squeezing every last drop from the precious daylight hours spent dancing up the rock face. Repetition is religion—he'll run the same routes over and over until each move, grip, and foothold is seared into his muscle memory.

His embodied mindset approach deserves equal praise. Honnold is an absolutely wonderful visualizer, mentally rehearsing every inch of the climb with crazy attention to detail. In his mind's eye, he can feel the rock's texture and anticipate each movement required to navigate the sketchiest sections. But he takes it even further by envisioning every possible scenario that could go sideways—the slips, precarious positions, and moments of doubt. He rehearses maintaining his cool under each with the same intensity as on the real rock, blurring the lines between imagination and reality. It's this profound mental discipline that allows him to stay focused when things get gnarly.

Still, climbing is just one part of Honnold's holistic embrace of rituals that prime him for the extraordinary. Before each ascent, he's got his own personal symphony of carefully crafted rituals—mental/physical warm-ups, stretching, and hydrating. These rituals roll out the pathway to a heightened state where every movement has an undeniable purpose.

And the rituals don't stop when the climbing does. Honnold understands the importance of processing the experience, integrating the lessons, and prepping for the next challenge through recovery practices. It's this cycle of preparation and reflection that keeps leveling him up.

In many ways, his approach mirrors other elite performers like alpine skier Mikaela Shiffrin, who ingrains every twist and roll into muscle memory with similar OCD-level attention to detail. It just reinforces that the principles governing peak performance transcend specific disciplines.

I don't recount Honnold's story just to highlight his supreme physical ability (though make no mistake, he is certainly a rock-climbing ninja). What really gets me is how his journey explores the mind-blowing potential we all have for hyperfocus, grit, and maybe even transcending our human limits.

Through his consistent commitment to finely crafted rituals, Honnold has elevated climbing to a graceful art form—a breathtaking dance upon the vertical world that leaves onlookers slack-jawed in awe. More than that, his example inspires me to embrace the extraordinary capabilities lying dormant within.

So, how does the man know when he's truly ready to step up for another mind-melting free solo link-up? It's not just about ticking the boxes on physical prep or technical ability. It's this holistic sense of preparedness, a deep intuitive knowing resonating through every fiber of his being—the confluence of supreme mental focus, physical expertise, and an unshakable trust in the power of his rituals.

For Honnold, the climb is simply an extension of the preparation, a seamless immersion in the flow he's already tapped into through his practice. Just like Shiffrin executes her runs with the naturalness of muscle memory, Honnold ascends with a profound awareness of every movement, sensation, and terrain nuance.

In those moments, fear and distraction are kicked to the curb, replaced by high focus transcending the physical act of climbing itself. Honnold becomes one with the rock, his movements a graceful symphony of precision, a sacred dance that few can even comprehend, let alone replicate.

This extraordinary ability isn't achieved overnight nor through mere natural talent. It's a life's work of unwavering dedication, relentless practice, and total commitment to rituals unlocking the extraordinary within.

Honnold's journey illustrates the transformative potential of the rituals, routines, and recovery practices we've explored throughout this chapter. His meticulous preparation, which involves intense physical training, mental rehearsal, and carefully crafted rituals, perfectly aligns with the key principles we've discussed.

But there's an even deeper connection here, one that ties back to the very heart of what it means to create a life of sustained embodied flow. Honnold's unwavering commitment to his rituals and routines isn't just about reaching the summit of El Capitan or any other specific climb. It's about the cumulative effect of showing up day after day, pouring every ounce of his being into the practices that shape him, inside and out. It's about the slow, steady work of becoming, of evolving into the best version of himself, one tiny improvement at a time.

And isn't that what this journey is all about for each of us? Whether we're crafting the perfect pre-game routine, fine-tuning our post-activity recovery practices, or experimenting with personalized flow triggers, we're all engaged in the sacred work of discovery and growth. We're all learning to embrace the power of rituals and routines to unlock the extraordinary potential that lies within us, waiting to be awakened.

So, let us take a page from Honnold's playbook and embrace the transformative mindset potential of these practices. Let us approach each day as an opportunity to show up fully, to pour ourselves into the rituals and routines that shape us.

Chapter 5:

How Embodied Flow Opens up Spaces of Possibility in Extreme Sports

At the outermost edges of human performance, extreme sports offer a phenomenological lens into radically expanded possibilities. Elite athletes here must fully immerse into a unified mind–body–environment condition of present-moment awareness, glimpsing untapped potentials awaiting their species.

Firsthand accounts from these rarified zones challenge conventional notions of control, stress, linear time, and rigid individuality. Rather than separations between being and environment, risk and rapture, these athletes describe an intuitive coalescence—a dissolving of subject–object boundaries into profound interconnectedness and responsiveness. In this heightened state of awareness, actions seem to flow effortlessly—a sense of timelessness, where the "past and future fade away, and the present moment becomes all-encompassing" (Dougall, 2023).

This exploration examines those pioneering lessons that could catalyze meaningful awakenings. Just as the first mapmakers expanded civilizations' horizons, today's experts of flow are charting new domains of possibility by remapping our cosmos of consciousness. By integrating such insights, we may access strategies for transcending cognitive isolation to unleash vastly expanded capacities in any endeavor.

Enacting Transformative Flow Potential

As athletes delve deeper into embodied flow, they can discover new levels of mind–body potential, inspiring them to conceive and execute increasingly audacious feats. These feats might include but are not limited to the following.

Attentional Focus

To engage in embodied flow is to immerse oneself fully into present-moment consciousness—at the core of this lies an extraordinary capacity for rapt, unwavering attention. In the extreme arenas where these athletes operate, even the slightest lapse in attentional focus could prove catastrophic. It is this intense stakes environment that allows them to master attentional stamina and commitment to the present moment that few can fathom.

Every fiber of one's being must be acutely attuned to the present reality, lest the consequences prove devastating. It is this total existential demand that allows us to glimpse the epitome of embodied presence. Those who choose to walk this razor's edge must bring every part of their being fully present—their skills, passion, strength, wisdom, perspective, and awareness—all integrated and engaged in the moment. Mind, body, and environment must be utterly and completely one. The present moment is all there is. The future is pure potential; the past is but a memory. This stark simplicity strips away the inessential and brings into laser focus what matters most—one's lived experience, right here and right now, in this instant.

There is no option to hold back or be distracted—you must bring every iota of focus and resolve to bear. There is also no room for delusion or minimizing risks, because that path leads only to suboptimal performance and missed opportunities.

Perceived Risk

Closely intertwined with these intense flow experiences is a heightened perception of risk. From there, their typical stress responses and perceived constraints around risk become transcended by a more profound awareness and responsiveness.

However, perceptual risk should not be misconstrued as a reckless disregard for safety. Rather, it is a calculated acceptance born from the clarity of embodied presence, coupled with meticulous preparation and risk mitigation strategies. Extreme athletes are acutely aware of the risks involved and take rigorous steps to minimize them through extensive training, careful planning, and adherence to safety protocols.

Just like Alex Hannold, wingsuit pilots, for example, who fly at breakneck speeds through narrow mountain ranges, spend countless hours honing their skills, studying terrains, and perfecting their equipment use to reduce the risk of fatal errors. This calculated approach to risk management allows extreme athletes to pursue their passions while maintaining a keen awareness of their own limitations and the potential consequences of their actions.

In the world of big mountain skiing, athletes like Jeremy Jones have developed a highly systematic approach to assessing and managing avalanche risk, one that involves a combination of advanced weather forecasting, terrain analysis, and snow science. By carefully studying the complex interplay of snowpack, weather patterns, and topography, these athletes are able to make informed decisions about when and where to ski, and how to navigate the complex and often unpredictable terrain of the high alpine environment.

Heightened Resilience

The very quest for sustained embodied flow forges extraordinary resilience capacities within extreme athletes too. Resilience, a multifaceted construct, encompasses not only the ability to bounce back from setbacks but also the capacity to thrive under challenging circumstances. Through their embodied experiences, extreme athletes cultivate remarkable mind–body toughness, grit, and adaptability, allowing them to persevere through physical, emotional, and environmental stressors.

Ultra-endurance athletes, such as those who compete in multiday adventure races, epitomize this resilience as they must endure grueling conditions, sleep deprivation, and extreme fatigue while maintaining laser focus and determination over incredibly extended periods.

A prime example is Courtney Dauwalter's record-setting performance at the 2022 Tahoe 200 Endurance Run, where she covered 205.5 mi in 92 hours and 10 minutes on technical mountain terrain (ISPO, n.d.). Dauwalter pushed through this multiday crucible taking only short naps while battling fatigue, altitude effects, and harsh weather. Yet, she dug deep to persevere: She stated that when her mind started working against her, she would bring it back to the present by telling it to focus on getting to the next aid station.

Similarly, adventure athlete Chrigel Maurer displayed incredible resilience in the 2021 X-Alps race, traversing approximately 750 km (466 miles) across the Alps by foot and paraglider (Red Bull X-Alps, 2021). He tackled over 32,000 meters of ascent while adhering to mandatory rest periods of only 4–5 hours per 24-hour period. Indeed, in the X-Alps, resilience is everything. You have to be prepared to fight through the depths of fatigue and pain, over and over, for days on end. It's about constantly renewing your motivation and digging so deep that you're operating on a different level mentally and physically.

In the realm of high-altitude mountaineering, climbers must overcome the debilitating effects of hypoxia, biting cold, and treacherous terrain, all while making life-or-death decisions under immense pressure. Conrad Anker, a renowned American mountaineer, has faced these challenges head-on. Anker himself has summited Everest three times, including once without supplemental oxygen.

In an interview, Anker described this experience as requiring a different approach compared to using supplemental oxygen (Gupta, 2024). He emphasized that climbing without supplemental oxygen is "a much slower process," and necessitates being "much more in tune with your body and your surroundings." This approach forces climbers to be deeply aware of their mind–body and the environment, making it a more profound and introspective experience compared to using supplemental oxygen.

Melissa Arnot, another accomplished American mountaineer, has also demonstrated remarkable resilience in the face of extreme conditions. She has summited Everest six times, more than any other American woman. In 2016, Arnot made history by completing the first successful ascent of Everest without supplemental oxygen by an American woman.

Reflecting on her achievement, Arnot stated,

> This has been an emotional journey, to say the least. Everest is an incredible mountain that continues to challenge and intrigue me. I never anticipated that I would be lucky enough to summit once, let alone six times. Climbing Everest without supplemental oxygen has been a goal of mine for a long time. When you succeed at reaching your goal, it makes you reflect on the hard days, the work, and the lessons I've learned along the way. I'm incredibly fortunate to have this experience. (Express Staff, 2016, paras. 6–7)

Nonetheless, the immersion into embodied flow does not merely enable heightened focus, perceptual risk, and resilience—it propels the continual refinement and expansion of the athlete's entire psychological repertoire. Their mental skill set is not static, but a proficiency constantly being honed and upgraded through the lived experiences that arise from deep embodied commitment.

As they push into increasingly rarified realms of unity and present-moment responsiveness, their intimate understanding of their own innate capacities and limitations evolves. Each plunge into embodied flow reveals new personal frontiers to transcend and integrate.

It is this iterative cycle—the continual expansion of consciousness realized through successive ebbs and flows in embodied experience, followed by deeper somatic awakenings and understandings—that allows for the nuanced refinement of techniques, strategies, and efficiency tools. With every profound immersion, the athletes access new terrains of being from which to handle the unknown challenges that inevitably arise from nature's intrinsic unpredictability.

Through the extraordinary examples of extreme athletes, we witness the immense transformative potential that can be unlocked by operating in intense present-moment embodied flow. Their feats of attentional focus, perceptual risk, resilience, and continual transcendence illuminate capacities that often lie dormant within us all.

However, the insights from their explorations need not remain rarified domains accessible only to a select few. Crucially, we need not remain spectators as their pioneering experiences can provide a blueprint for our own journey.

In the following section, we draw insights from their deep immersion in intense present-moment consciousness to develop an elevated mind–body and actualize new layers of our innate potential. The paths of these extreme athletes light the way for any of us to fully inhabit the present, embrace uncertainties as opportunities, and continually refine our mastery of the embodied-flow mindset. The realm of embodied flow births powerful possibilities—it is up to us to courageously explore them.

Embodying Flow Mindset in Extreme Sports

For extreme athletes, the cultivation of embodied flow is the result of a deliberate and disciplined approach that encompasses physical conditioning, technical skill development, and crucial mind–body mindset training. While physical prowess and technical mastery lay the foundation, it is the athlete's mind–body mindset that ultimately determines their ability to access embodied flow and perform at the highest levels consistently.

As shared by Adel Honi, professional paragliding pilot,

> Flying is 80% mental. Whatever I improve in the technical aspect is only going to improve 20% of my game. The technical

stuff only makes a very small difference in my flying. But when I learned about modeling success; visualization; using a mantra while flying; learning to deal with fears; how to set appropriate goals; dealing with failure; working on my self-confidence; meditation; choosing a mentor... when I started analyzing all these things, my flying took huge leaps. I was ranked in the top 200 in the world, when I only had about 600 hours. And I'm completely average. I'm not very athletic and I'm not particularly talented as a pilot. Anyone can do this. Psychology is huge in this sport. (McClurg, 2021, p. 23)

The next section delves into the critical mind–body mindset strategies employed by elite extreme athletes to heighten awareness and catalyze embodied flow.

Mind–Body Mindset Strategies for Peak Performance

Reframing Perceptual Possibility

Fear is a natural response when you're staring down a 100-ft big wave, looking over the edge of a cliff you're about to jump off, or stepping up to the starting line of an ultramarathon through the mountains. Too much fear and anxiety can be paralyzing and dangerous. But a little fear can actually help by sharpening your focus and flooding your body with adrenaline. As Jeb Corliss, one of the world's top wingsuit pilots, learned after a near-fatal crash in 2012, losing fear entirely can be deadly. "I made a big mistake. I lost fear," he admitted (McClurg, 2021).

This means there should be a delicate balance between fear and performance, which can be achieved through various techniques.

1. Cognitive Restructuring

Cognitive restructuring is a technique that helps athletes reframe their relationship with fear.

Think about it this way: When you try to forcefully block out or eliminate fear, you're still giving it prime mental real estate. The more you fight it, the more you feed it. It's like a wrestling match where the more you grapple with the fear, the stronger its hold becomes.

The alternative is a practiced form of acceptance. Not begrudging acceptance out of hopeless resignation. But an evolved acceptance that comes from clearly seeing fear's nature and role.

From this perspective, fear is neither ignored nor indulged. It's acknowledged as the embodied reality check that you're stepping into a realm of legitimate consequence.

So, the first step is to get exquisitely comfortable witnessing anxiety or stress without hostility. Just notice the prickly sensations, the looping thoughts, the adrenaline rushes. Meet their intensity with an open curiosity rather than forceful resistance.

As you practice this mirroring awareness, a remarkable transition starts to occur. Anxiety concerns charged energy no longer snowballs into overwhelming dread. It's just there, like background music waiting to be reinterpreted. You remain collected as the frontmost part of your consciousness. Then, the mind–body reframing can follow.

Many athletes describe feeling the fear manifesting as a tightness in their gut, their heart racing. Rather than trying to push it away, they consciously breathe into that sensation, giving it space to be there. With steady, accepting breaths, they almost dance with the fear, letting it surge and ebb without judging it. Strangely, after a point, the concentrated ball of anxiety often starts to diffuse into a more expansive hyperawareness.

From this relaxed awareness, the greatest performers can logically reassess the risks and opportunities. They don't arrogantly dismiss fear's reality checks, but they also don't subconsciously catastrophize like the doomsayers. Their evaluations turn more measured, creative, and adaptive to changing conditions.

Most importantly, there is no time for emotion or perceptual stress and anxiety, as this interferes with embodied flow for the body-mind-environment interaction.

2. Comprehensive Preparation and Perceptual Training

One of the biggest sources of perceptual fear is the unknown—not knowing what obstacles or dangers lie ahead. When the mind–body encounters this void of uncertainty, it tends to fill it with vivid imaginations of potential threats, fueling anxiety. Given that, nothing helps quell perceptual fear like knowing you're as prepared as possible. Endless hours of mind–body training, visualizing every possible scenario, and taking every safety precaution instills confidence and embodied preparation.

Chrigel Maurer, a living embodiment of this ethos, has carved a legendary path through his comprehensive approach, leaving an indelible mark on the world of paragliding.

Maurer's dedication to integrated mind–body preparation is unparalleled. He meticulously envisions every aspect of his daring feats, from the intricate route lines to the potential obstacles that may arise, while simultaneously conditioning his mind–body to execute each movement with unwavering precision. This mental rehearsal is seamlessly interwoven with his physical training, allowing him to orchestrate each action with a profound unity of intention and execution.

Through his holistic approach, Maurer builds an unwavering core strength that transcends mere muscular power. He hones his mind–body to maintain stable positioning even in the most precarious situations, transforming his entire presence into a finely tuned resonance capable of defying gravity's relentless grip. Every cell and sinew of his being is conditioned to respond with a singular, unwavering focus, exemplifying the epitome of mastering embodied flow mindset.

Another approach that sets Maurer apart is his uncompromising approach to safety. He adheres to stringent protocols, personally inspecting and packing his parachutes and equipment before each flight (Maurer, 2016).

Of course, you also should trust—deeply trust—yourself, your training, and your equipment. Elite athletes like Maurer have fostered an invaluable faith in their abilities honed over years of dedicated work. When they prepare for flight, there is zero questioning of whether their mind–bodies are ready.

3. Achieving Total Mind–Body Absorption

The ability to attune fully to the dynamic unfolding of the present moment, achieving total mind–body absorption, is critical for extreme athletes to overcome perceptual stress to achieve peak performance. When your life's on the line, you can't afford even the slightest fracture in present-moment focus. All that matters is the next hold, the next turn, the next breath—an unwavering unity of mind and body acting as one coherent embodiment of attention. As Chrigel Maurer says, "It sounds strange, but when I do intense events like the X-Alps, I really focus on the moment. There is nothing else. As long as I can focus on the problem, I can compete" (McClurg, 2021).

Or as BASE jumper Steph Davis described her experience jumping from the 876-ft-tall Kjeragbolten boulder in Norway:

> You're never not going to be scared. I'm scared every time I do a base jump. Every time you get close to the edge, you feel it, whether it's just a little bit and you just think "OK, I feel a little intensity" or you're actually scared. You always feel that. The thing is to figure out how to manage it and make sure it's not controlling you physically because that's the only time there's a problem with fear—when it's kind of handicapping you physically, but the fact that it makes you extra alert, extra cautious, really aware of everything, that's really important. (Miller, 2013, para. 4)

However, achieving and sustaining this level of rapt, unbroken mind–body absorption does not come easily, even for elites. It requires years of dedicated mind–body training to intricately interweave one's mental focus with physical immersion in the task. Just as they drill techniques into muscle memory, athletes must intentionally practice and refine this mind–body unity.

This involves constantly bringing attention back to evaluating one's current condition of mind–body concentration during all activities.

Over time, these integrated moments of mind–body experience may become second nature, fortifying the athlete's ability to achieve profound embodied flow when it matters most. It is this skill that allows the extraordinary to be treated as routine evolving present peak performance moments.

Another trick that extreme athletes often employ to maintain focus over longer stretches of grueling multiday events is breaking things down into small, manageable chunks and just focusing on nailing one piece at a time. If you run across the Great Himalaya Trail, it's best to forget about the total distance of 1,056 mi.

As ultra-endurance athlete and adventurer Michael Strasser says in an interview with Red Bull: "That's the crux of the matter. I don't ride 300 km in one day—I divide it in my head into three parts, so I only ride 100 km three times," he explains (Baumgartner, 2020). "I can grasp this distance and, mentally, I have a point of reference for my training," he continues. Strasser also uses a system of rewards to maintain his motivation: "After each 100km, I try to give myself a reward, like an energy bar. In this way, I'm kind of trying to dangle a carrot in front of my own nose" (Baumgartner, 2020). This approach not only makes the daunting task feel more achievable but also provides frequent positive reinforcement, which is vital for sustaining endurance and performance over long distances.

All you should think about is reaching the next checkpoint or village. One foot in front of the other, one day at a time. The ability to maintain that level of presence and focus for weeks on end takes a lot of training, but it can tap into some deep reservoirs of mental strength and endurance.

When I'm thermaling, I focus solely on the move I'm currently working on. I know that I must earn each move to make my next move simple. It's all about taking it one step at a time, focusing on getting around the route 1 km at a time, not thinking about the entire 100 km journey ahead. I concentrate on nailing each individual thermal, each kilometer of the route. I trust that by stringing together these small victories, I'll ultimately complete the entire flight successfully.

Of course, despite an athlete's best efforts to stay fully present in the moment, there will be times when perceptual anxiety manages to pierce through that focus. When these perceptions arise to fracture their focus, the athletes do not fight it through willpower alone. Instead, they lean into the mind–body connection. They tune into the somatic signals—muscle tension, rapid breathing, and sweaty palms—the body's early warning systems. Then they use holistic techniques like controlled breathing, positive self-talk, and vivid visualization to recenter themselves.

Personal rituals and routines can also initiate the switch into a state of hyperlucid flow when high-stakes moments arrive. It could be something as simple as Alex Honnold meticulously chalking up his hands before a demanding rock climb, or a skier snapping their goggles before dropping into a big line. These little rituals and talismans are highly personal, but they can make a real difference.

For me, these rituals are intimately tied to the different phases of my flight. While flying, I might take a bite of a protein bar on glide or focus on deep breaths to calm my mind–body. I also make a point of shaking out my arms and ensuring that I'm relaxed in my harness, which allows me to better feel the subtle shifts in the air. Depending on whether I'm in thermaling mode, gliding mode, or planning my next move, my focus and rituals adapt.

I've even gone so far as to write reminders on my flight deck, like "BREATHE," or whatever reminders to prompt me to ask myself, *Will this move put me on the ground?* before making it and listening to my gut for each question. These little prompts help me stay centered and make confident decisions in the moment, trusting my instincts and responding to each movement of the air with the appropriate inputs to keep my risers even on glide and carve smoothly through thermals.

4. Fostering a Deep Connection With the Environment

For extreme athletes, cultivating a deep connection with the natural world is not just a byproduct of their pursuits, but a fundamental aspect of their ability to handle challenges and achieve embodied flow. This deep attunement to the environment allows them to read the subtle cues and rhythms of their surroundings, making split-second decisions that can mean the difference between success and failure.

Across various disciplines, extreme athletes emphasize the importance of developing an intimate understanding of the environment they navigate. In the world of big-wave surfing, surfers like Shane Dorian speak of the need to cultivate a "sixth sense" for the water. "You have to be able to read the ocean, to understand the swell direction, the tide, the wind. It's all about [the] experience and being in tune with nature," Dorian explains in interviews with *The Surfer's Journal* and *Towsurfer* (Brisickl, 2024; Akiskalian, 2004; Jarvis, 2017). "When you're out there, it's about feeling the wave, knowing when to go and when to wait. It's a split-second decision that can make all the difference" (Jarvis, 2017).

Similarly, wingsuit pilot Jeb Corliss, known for his death-defying flights through narrow canyons and mountain ranges, stresses the importance of "feeling the air" (Shah, 2017). He emphasizes that the most crucial aspect of wingsuit flying is understanding and respecting air currents. It's a constant dance with the environment, where one must be completely aware and adaptive to the changing conditions. Corliss explains:

> When you knowingly place yourself in extreme danger, where a mistake means certain death, your mind enters a unique space. For instance, during intense base jumps, you stand on the edge, every fibre of your being screaming not to leap. But once you commit, once you step off, there's a paradigm shift. Your body, having resisted so fiercely, suddenly releases a cocktail of chemicals to help you perform at your peak. The past and future blur; only the present matters. You're so engrossed in the moment that it becomes your entire world. (Shah, 2017, para. 16)

For high-altitude mountaineers, the connection with the environment is a matter of survival. As mountaineer Ed Viesturs puts it, "The mountain decides whether you climb or not. The art of mountaineering is knowing when to go, when to stay, and when to retreat. Getting to the top is optional. Getting down is mandatory" (Viesturs & Roberts, 2011).

To develop this deep connection with the environment, extreme athletes engage in a variety of practices that help them tune into the present moment and open up to the subtle cues and energies of their surroundings. The surfer, for example, immerses themselves in the study of ocean conditions. They study the conditions obsessively, examining weather maps, swell models, and wind forecasts. They visualize the wave, the line they'll take, and how the water will feel. For them, it's a constant process of observation and adaptation.

Likewise, the wingsuit flier dedicates significant time to understanding the terrain and weather patterns they'll encounter during flights. They thoroughly study the landscape, weather patterns, and air currents. Visualizing the flight path repeatedly, they anticipate every possible scenario. While in the air, they continuously read the environment, sensing wind movements and making split-second adjustments.

The mountaineer's preparation involves meticulous study of weather maps and mountain condition reports, as well as gathering information from fellow climbers. On the mountain, they constantly observe weather changes, snow conditions, and shifts in light. Their experience is an ongoing process of interpreting the environment and making informed decisions based on these observations.

In addition to these specific practices, extreme athletes may also engage in meditation or breath work to quiet the chatter of the mind and sharpen their focus, or simply spend time in nature, observing the play of light and shadow, the movement of wind and water, and the subtle shifts in energy and atmosphere.

On days when cross-country flights are impractical due to unfavorable conditions, I dedicate my time to honing my skills in various ways— ones that deepen my connection to the air and enhance my embodied flow. I practice feeling the air, refining my thermaling accuracy, and discovering the intricate movements of air currents. I study thermal edges and observe how wind bends thermals based on factors like humidity, pressure, and solar energy. It's fascinating to learn from the birds themselves, watching how they use their wings to navigate the skies, silently showing me the way.

Learning and practicing are always at the forefront of my mind. My appetite for knowledge in this field is insatiable, and I'm constantly amazed by the possibilities that unfold with each new discovery. Every moment in the air, whether it's a long-distance flight or a practice session, offers an opportunity to deepen my understanding of the complex dance between pilot, craft, and the ever-changing atmosphere.

Understanding the Paradox of Effortless Effort for Peak Performance

The great paradox underlying all transcendent performance, all experiences of flow under the spotlight's blinding fire, is that the more desperately we try to force flow, the more elusive it becomes. The sort of hyperfocused, ecstatic union with our craft that iconic athletes open arises not from willful strain, but from an almost childlike letting go into the currents of creative emergence experience.

As the French phenomenological philosopher Merleau-Ponty (1964) illuminates, the very structure of human bodily experience involves an inherent organizing intelligence—an innate dynamism surpassing our conscious will yet guiding our most exquisite physical expressions. When an expert performer like Federer, the iconic Swiss tennis champion, glides across the court, his fluid excellence materializes not from controlling each micromovement through sheer force of focused intent. Rather, his artistry flows as the organic byproduct of years of dedicated attunement—refining proprioceptive sensitivity until his being resonates as one seamless mind–body instrument playing the music of reality itself (Dreyfus, 2005).

Or when Jornet runs, he emphasizes:

> At the moment you are able to take away any emotion, then you are ready. If you have euphoria or are happy, you are more

likely to make bad decisions because you will not see all the risks. If you are scared, you will panic or start to lose control. You need to be able to ask yourself if you can technically and physically do the climb. If you can, you can evaluate the true risk and make a rational decision. The only way to get to this point is to spend hours and hours preparing for these situations. It's a sort of meditation, but you come out with more knowledge for future experiences (Graepel, 2017, para. 18).

Jornet is the renowned Spanish trail runner and multirecord holder in distances like the Ultra-Trail du Mont-Blanc.

Letting Go to Allow Flow's Arising

There is profound wisdom in learning to surrender the metaphysics of control itself—to cease grasping so the deeper orders of spontaneous perfection can unfurl through us. This path of "order from noise" may seem paradoxical, but it echoes through every tradition of enacting embodied flow.

From the Zen archery of Eugen Herrigel relinquishing all motived efforts to let the arrow "shoot itself," to Carse's insights on infinite, unselfconscious play versus the finite games of forced intention—we see this theme emerge again and again. An unconditioned openness, a letting go, precedes and supports the uncanny breakthroughs where time and embodied movement dissolve into unified flow.

Some extreme athletes and performing artists—those who cling to outward ideals of "perfect" technique, who grip their instruments or disciplines through sheer willpower—inevitably struggle to stabilize flow possibilities. Meanwhile, those who've softened attachment to outcome, who remain permeable and creatively responsive within the arising challenges, seem to slip into hyperlucid absorption with striking poise and consistency. I believe the only way to get what you really want from high performance or to enjoy the journey is to stop craving it so intensely.

Chapter 6:

Designing an Embodied-Flow

Practice

For many of us, the path to embodied flow feels tantalizingly out of reach. We experience fleeting moments of it—during an exhilarating workout, a burst of creative inspiration, or when deeply immersed in a challenging task. Yet we often struggle to reliably access it when we need it most. How, then, do we bridge the gap between these ephemeral experiences and a life of sustained excellence?

To illuminate this path, we turn to one of the world's foremost experts on peak performance and embodied flow—coach Thomas Theurillat. Having worked with extreme athletes like Chrigel Maurer, top businesses such as Swiss Re and Nestlé, and individuals, including members of the Tonhalle Orchestra Zürich, seeking to attain their highest potential on demand, Theurillat has developed a transformative approach to designing personalized flow practices.

At the heart of Theurillat's approach lies a deceptively simple tool: the power of asking the right questions. He believes that through deep inquiry and reflection, we can uncover the unique conditions that allow us to access embodied flow. It's not about following a one-size-fits-all formula, but rather embarking on a journey of discovery to understand our own triggers, challenges, and optimal performance zones.

This personalized approach is crucial because embodied flow is inherently individual. As Theurillat explains, "How can I advise someone who knows much more about who they are than I do? I only ask questions. I never told Chrigel what I thought he should do; I just asked him questions and let him decide" (McClurg, 2021). What catalyzes flow for one person may completely disrupt it for another. By designing a practice tailored to your specific needs, strengths, and goals, you dramatically increase your chances of consistently accessing peak performance.

In this chapter, we'll explore Theurillat's innovative framework for crafting your own embodied-flow practice. Whether you're an athlete looking to shatter personal records, a professional aiming to skyrocket your productivity and innovation, or simply someone who wants to infuse each day with more purpose and vitality, this chapter holds the keys to unlocking your extraordinary potential.

Envisioning Your Peak Performance Potential

The journey to embodied flow begins with a clear vision of your peak performance potential. This process of envisioning isn't just daydreaming—it's a powerful tool for priming your mind–body for success. Believe it or not, what your mind can conceive and believe, it can push past your perceived limitations to achieve.

To harness this transformative energy effectively, we'll explore several key strategies that can help you create a vivid, actionable vision of your peak performance. These include recognizing patterns of successes, time jump exercises, crafting detailed narratives of your ideal performance, and developing contingency planning. Each of these approaches offers a unique way to tap into your potential and prepare your mind–body system for exceptional achievement.

Recognizing Patterns of Success in Peak Performance

To identify patterns of success, let's start by listing your top 10 successes. Take a moment to reflect on times when you've performed at your best. For each performance, ask yourself

- What specific actions did I take during this experience?

- How did I feel?

- In what ways did this performance differ from my previous experiences? Were there any notable improvements or challenges? If so, how did I address them?

- What were the weather conditions like on the day of this event? Did they have any impact on my performance?

- How was my mind–body condition during the performance? Did I feel well-prepared, focused, and in sync with my body, mind, and environment?

- What were my overall performance metrics?

- Were there any critical decisions I made during the experience that significantly influenced the outcome?

When Thomas asks pilots to list their top successes, he often encourages them to dedicate an entire evening to analyzing their 10 best flights, as he wants them to consider it as more than just a quick recall. Rather, it's homework, an analysis laid out on a spreadsheet. This meticulous approach provides a deeper understanding of the conditions and factors contributing to their peak performance.

Thanks to this method, several individuals have discovered their own success patterns. Some have reported that they perform their best when away from home, perhaps because they are on holiday or far from work stress. Meanwhile, others excel in technically challenging flights with weak conditions.

After all, consistent successes need to be the result of formulating a customized plan that makes the most of your distinct abilities and situational factors.

By approaching peak performance as a replicable pattern rather than a matter of chance or innate talent, we can move from hoping for success to systematically creating the conditions for it. As Thomas said, "If you look at people who win repeatedly over several years, it's only because they have created a successful pattern" (McClurg, 2021).

In my own experience, I've found that recognizing patterns of success often involves adhering to key principles and adapting them to specific situations. Two concepts from Kelly Farina's *Mastering Paragliding* have been particularly influential in my approach: "Discard what doesn't serve" and "Earn a move to make a move."

For example, if the area ahead is shaded or the wind picks up in a quadrant of the sky, it's time to discard and adopt a new route for the day. Also, if I haven't earned the height needed to make a crossing, I have to stay where I am until a thermal or the sun comes back so I can get the needed height to make a crossing and stay in the "cone of advantage for flying the day." Since we don't have engines, we have to decisively make decisions based on our patterns of success recognition and know when to stop and earn the move; otherwise, the next decision could put you on the ground since you don't have an engine.

Time Jump Exercise

The time jump exercise is a powerful visualization technique that has been effective for many athletes, including Yael Margelisch, a Swiss pilot who started working with coach Thomas Theurillat 5 years ago to overcome her lack of confidence and self-doubt.

Margelisch is a remarkable athlete with numerous achievements in paragliding. She started flying at the age of 19 and is now an Ozone team pilot, flying the Enzo 3. Margelisch is well-known for her world records, including the current FAI Triangle record of 263 km in the Swiss Alps. In October 2019, she broke the women's world distance record previously held by Marcelo Prieto, a Brazilian pilot who flew 442.1 km in Brazil. About 10 days later, she flew an impressive 531 km from Caico to Pau dos Ferros, Brazil, making her the only woman to have flown over 500 km and setting a new women's world record.

Despite her incredible achievements, Margelisch struggled with confidence and doubt for many years. She often thought she wasn't doing well enough and would degrade herself. As she explains,

> I had problems with self-confidence, so really being sure of myself and knowing what I can do and so on. He [Thomas] really helped me this way to set my goals and to get to see what

was important to get to a good performance mode so it's a good flow. (McClurg, 2020)

The time jump exercise involves the following steps:

- To begin the exercise, close your eyes and imagine yourself at the starting line of your chosen event or performance. This could be hours (e.g., 2 hours before the event), days (e.g., the morning of the event), months (e.g., 1 month before a major competition), or even years (e.g., visualizing yourself at the Olympics in 4 years). Take a moment to fully immerse yourself in the environment, noticing the details around you and the sensations in your mind–body.

- Next, "jump" forward in time to the finish line, having completed the perfect performance. Visualize yourself executing each stage of the event flawlessly, and pay attention to the feelings of confidence, focus, and flow that accompany this ideal outcome.

- Now, turn around and look back at the course or event you just completed. Observe the details of your perfect performance. What key actions or decisions did you make along the way that led to this success? Then, tune into the mind–body sensations you experienced along the way. Which emotions are you experiencing in this imagined future? Allow yourself to fully feel the satisfaction, pride, and joy of your accomplishment.

- Finally, "float" back in time to place yourself at the starting line once again. Only now, you carry with you the knowledge and embodied experience of having already achieved your goal. Feel the confidence and certainty that comes from knowing you have what it takes to perform at your peak.

To maximize the effectiveness of this visualization method, it is crucial to engage all your senses and fully immerse yourself in the emotional experience of success. Simply put, you need to live it, experientially enacting every moment. The more you can be in and embody the experience, the more deeply the success you've envisioned will become ingrained in your mind–body system.

Before her record-breaking flights, Theurillat used his question-based approach to have Margelisch explain what she wanted to say after the record flight before she left for Brazil. "If you really challenge people to explain their dream, then it is very interesting to see how they will use their strength," he said (McClurg, 2021). Clearly, he is correct in believing that when we know what the perfect day looks like, we can start preparing for it.

Crafting Detailed Success Stories

Dr. Daniel Gucciardi, a renowned sports psychologist, has extensively researched the use of narrative techniques in mind–body preparation. His work reveals that athletes who engage in storytelling as part of their visualization process often experience enhanced imagery and improved performance outcomes (Gucciardi et al., 2010).

This narrative approach to visualization goes beyond simple mind–body rehearsal. It involves crafting a detailed, perceptually rich story of your ideal performance. By engaging in this process, you're not just seeing success in your eyes; you're creating a multisensory, deeply personal account that can serve as a powerful blueprint for your mind–body system.

Here's how to craft your narrative success visualization:

- **Set the stage:** Begin your story by describing the setting in vivid detail. Where are you? What time of day is it? What's the weather like? Engage all your senses (e.g., "The crisp morning air fills my lungs as I stand at the starting line. The sun is just peeking over the horizon, casting a golden glow across the racecourse. I can smell the dew on the grass and hear the quiet murmur of anticipation from the crowd").

- **Introduce the protagonist (You):** Describe yourself in this moment. How do you feel? What are you thinking? (e.g., "I feel strong, my muscles coiled with potential energy. My mind–body is focused solely on the task ahead. A sense of calm confidence washes over me—I know I'm prepared for this moment").

- **The journey begins:** Detail the start of your performance. What are your first actions? How does your mind–body respond? What's your initial strategy? (e.g., "As the starting gun fires, I explode into action. My first strides are powerful and controlled. I settle quickly into my rhythm, my breathing steady and strong").

- **Overcoming challenges:** Include obstacles in your narrative and how you overcome them. This mental problem-solving can be crucial for real-world adaptability (e.g., "Halfway through, I hit the dreaded hill. My legs begin to burn, but I embrace the discomfort. I recall my training, leaning slightly forward and pumping my arms. With each step, I visualize myself getting stronger, leaving my competitors behind").

- **The climax:** Describe the peak moment of your performance in rich detail. What does success look and feel like? (e.g., "As I round the final corner, I see the finish line. With a surge of adrenaline, I increase my pace. The cheers of the crowd blend into white noise as I focus entirely on those last few meters. I cross the line with my arms raised, a mix of elation and relief flooding through me").

- **The aftermath:** Include how you feel after your success and its impact. This reinforces the positive attitudes associated with your achievement (e.g., "As I catch my breath, a sense of pride and accomplishment washes over me. I've not just won the race, I've conquered my own doubts and pushed beyond what I thought possible. This victory is a stepping stone to even greater achievements").

Practice writing and revising your success story regularly. As you progress in your training and gain new insights, update your narrative to reflect your evolving goals and perception. This living document becomes not just a visualization tool, but a record of your growth and a constant source of motivation.

As you engage in this narrative success visualization, you're not just preparing for a single event—you're crafting the story of the athlete you're becoming. This process can profoundly shape your identity and approach to your sport, setting the stage for sustained peak performance.

Pro tips: When crafting your detailed vision, it's best to

1. Write in the present tense to create immediacy.

2. Include sensory details from all five senses.

3. Describe your emotions throughout the performance.

4. Visualize vividly overcoming potential obstacles.

5. Enacting each peak performance moment over and over as if it's real.

Developing Contingency Planning

Contingency planning matters precisely because of the weather's unpredictability. It prepares you to be open to the possibilities of the changing situation. Simply put, nature is changeable, so you have to prepare for change too.

Do not misunderstand; contingency planning is not about trying to predict or control these changes. This approach doesn't make sense and is often futile. Instead, it's about being prepared for whatever situations arise. It means having the right equipment, strategies, and, most crucially, the mind–body flexibility to adapt swiftly. One day, you may battle through relentless rain, maneuvering across slippery trails with limited visibility. The next, you might face scorching heat, putting your endurance and hydration strategies to the test. Each phase demands a different approach, different gear, and a different mindset.

So, without planning for various scenarios beforehand, you aren't able to transition seamlessly as conditions shift. A sudden weather change can derail you if you haven't already considered how to respond. This poor preparedness may then prevent you from maintaining peak performance.

How to Create Your Own Contingency Plans

Creating effective contingency plans involves several key steps. Below is a detailed guide to help you develop your own strategic plans for any situation.

Identify Potential Scenarios

Begin by brainstorming all possible scenarios you might encounter. This includes best-case, worst-case, and most-likely situations. Consider specific challenges and opportunities each scenario presents, which may involve

- environmental factors (e.g., wind changes, sudden storms, shaded areas, temperature fluctuations, and terrain variations)

- equipment issues (e.g., gear failure, performance issues, loss, damage, need for backup equipment, equipment limitations and constraints, and adaptability to changing equipment requirements)

- mind–body challenges (e.g., fatigue, injury, altitude sickness, resetting focus, overwhelming pressure, or eating/drinking/energy management)

- external factors (e.g., competitor strategies and course changes)

Develop Multiple Plans

1. **Approach A (Optimal conditions):** This plan is your preferred strategy when conditions are perfect.

   o Outline your ideal strategy for perfect conditions.

   o Specify performance targets and key milestones.

   o Detail your optimal pacing and energy management approach.

- List required resources and equipment.

- Identify critical decision points and success criteria.

2. **Approach B (Moderate conditions):** A backup plan for when conditions are not ideal but still manageable.

    - Address the most likely disruptions to Plan A.

    - Incorporate alternative routes or strategies.

    - Specify trigger points for switching from Plan A to B.

    - Outline modified performance expectations.

    - Detail resource reallocation and energy conservation methods.

    - Describe communication protocols with your support team or coach.

3. **Approach C (Adverse conditions):** A fallback plan for when conditions are challenging or dangerous.

    - Focus on risk mitigation and damage control strategies.

    - Redefine success criteria for extremely challenging conditions.

    - Detail emergency procedures and safety protocols.

    - Specify minimum performance goals.

    - Outline crisis communication plans.

    - Describe methods for preserving energy and resources for future opportunities.

Prepare Your Mind–Body

- Use the time jump visualization technique to rehearse each plan.

- Practice transitioning between plans during training sessions.

- Develop specific mindfulness techniques for staying calm and maintaining focus under pressure.

Stay Flexible

- Identify key decision points where you'll reassess your strategy.

- Develop a checklist for quickly evaluating changing conditions.

- Practice making rapid decisions under simulated pressure.

Evaluate and Adjust

After each performance or training session

- Conduct a thorough debrief, analyzing the effectiveness of your plans.

- Identify any unforeseen challenges and how you addressed them.

- Update your plans based on new insights and experiences.

Ultimately, the goal of contingency planning is to make you resilient and adaptable for the best performance. As long as you have plan B and C in your head, you can focus on plan A. So when plan A is not working, you will not be stressed out because you have a good plan B and C. This way, you can switch directly without having to think about it. As Chrigel Maurer (2020) said: "Thinking in the air needs time, and normally the solutions under pressure are not good. So, I always say,

'Think about plan B and C faster and easier once you have good options.'"

Speaking of Chrigel Maurer, I have to admit that the strategies to develop proficient contingency plans you've just learned are inspired by the writings on his gloves. Like Maurer, I've adopted this innovative approach, writing my own strategies on the fingers of my gloves, as well as adding a few cockpit deck reminders. These tactile cues are invaluable aids, promoting calm efficiency in flight and ensuring that critical information is literally at my fingertips when I need it most.

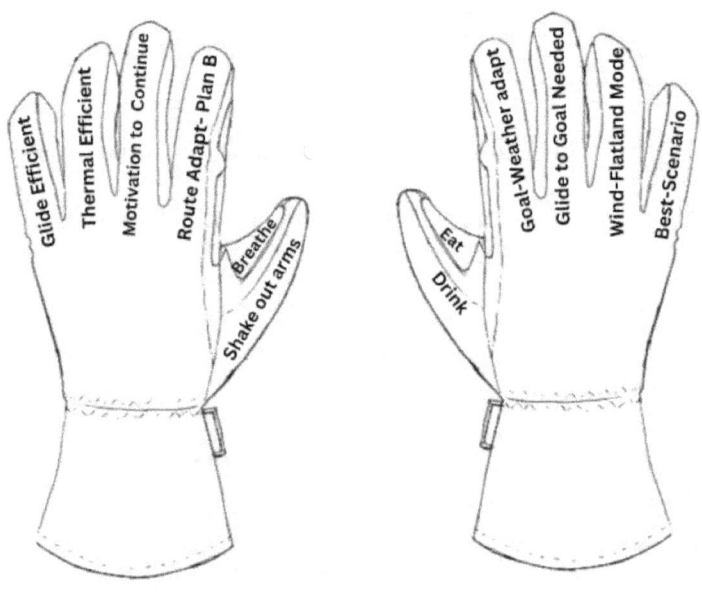

Building Your Performance Toolkit for Peak Performance

In the pursuit of embodied flow, having the right strategic tools can make all the difference. Just as a master craftsman relies on a well-curated set of instruments, peak performers need a versatile toolbox to pick out the right tool for the job to maneuver the complexities of high-level performance.

Circle of Control

The circle of control concept helps you differentiate what you can directly control, what you can influence, and what lies beyond your reach (Covey, 1989). By understanding and applying this tool, you can focus your energy and attention on the areas where you can make the most impact, ultimately leading to mastery of potential.

The circle of control includes three main circles:

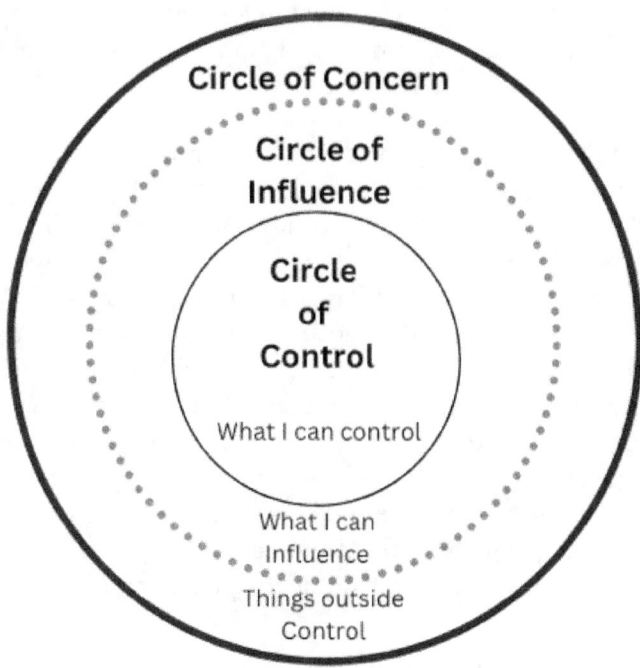

- **Circle of control:** This is the innermost circle. It's all about you—your thoughts, actions, and reactions. You have direct control over these things. For example, you can control how much effort you put into training, what you eat, or how you respond to nature which doesn't care who you are. Focusing here can be incredibly empowering. Because when you zero in on the things you can directly control, you have an unshakable confidence in yourself and your abilities. You know exactly what you need to do to succeed, you have a clear vision of what success looks like, and you have a strong focus on making it happen. You know that you've put in the work—that your mind–body is ready for the experiential challenges for optimal performance.

- **Circle of influence:** This is the middle circle. It includes things you can affect but don't have complete control over, like your relationships, your work projects, or your team's performance. At its core, the circle of influence is about recognizing that you're part of something bigger than yourself. As an athlete, you're not just a solo performer—you're part of a complex web of relationships, systems, and influences that shape your experience and your success.

- **Circle of concern:** This is the outermost ring. It contains all the things that you might worry about or be concerned with, but that you have little to no direct control over. For extreme sports athletes, this could include factors like the weather conditions on competition day, the performance of your competitors, or the judging or scoring system. It's natural to have concerns about these external factors. After all, they basically take us out of embodied flow and consume valuable energy for resetting, reframing, or evolving to the constantly changing moments. If the weather turns, or there's unexpected shading during key times—like siesta hours—it can throw off my whole paragliding flight, especially if I haven't reached the right terrain to maintain altitude in light lift conditions.

Applying the Circle of Control

1. **Identify and list:** Take time to identify and list factors in each circle for your specific sport or performance area.

2. **Focus your energy:** Concentrate your efforts on your circle of control. These are the areas where your actions have the most direct impact.

3. **Leverage your influence:** For items in your circle of influence, develop strategies to maximize your positive impact while acknowledging the limits of your control.

4. **Let go:** Practice accepting the factors in your circle of concern. Develop coping strategies to minimize their impact on your performance without wasting energy trying to control them.

5. **Regular review:** Periodically reassess your circles. As you grow and develop, you may find that some items shift between circles.

Spiral of Success

The spiral of success framework leverages the concept of small wins to build momentum and create a sense of progress. It's a simple but effective idea: By setting achievable goals and celebrating each victory along the way, athletes can create an upward trajectory that propels them toward success.

When faced with a significant challenge, it's common to feel overwhelmed. However, if you break that challenge down into smaller, more manageable pieces, you can create a roadmap for success that feels attainable and rewarding. Each small practice step once embodied through lots and lots of focused experience becomes the building block for embodied flow success.

Hitting a goal, no matter how modest, proves to yourself that progress is possible. You begin to see yourself as someone who can overcome obstacles and achieve great things. This shift in perception is crucial, as it reinforces the belief in your own abilities and potential. It's a virtuous cycle that can lead to remarkable breakthroughs and personal bests.

Peak Performance Potential

Technique Embodied

Small Goal Wins

Decisions on Point

Flow

Shift in Perception

Efficiency Breakthroughs

Achieve Success

Skill Achievements

Triangle of Change

The pursuit of excellence is an ongoing journey. We continually strive to reach new heights, refine our skills, and enhance our mind–body connection for peak performance. This isn't about change in the traditional sense—we're not trying to change who you are, but rather foster your embodied growth mindset, resilience, and adaptability.

The triangle of change with its three elements—desire, strength, and action—is a powerful framework for this pursuit.

- **Desire:** This is the starting point of any change. It's the spark that ignites the process. This internal motivation comes from recognizing the need for change and envisioning a better future. A strong desire is needed to achieve peak performance.

- **Strength:** This is the "fuel" that sustains the embodied transformational change process. It's not just about physical prowess. It's the resilience and inner resources that keep us going when the initial excitement wanes or when obstacles arise. As we've explored, struggle often precedes our breakthrough into embodied flow. Recognizing this pattern helps us push through challenges, knowing they're stepping stones to our peak performance. Strength can come from various sources—personal determination, support systems, acquired skills, or past experiences of overcoming difficulties.

- **Action:** These are the concrete steps we take toward the envisioned change. This involves planning—breaking down the big goal into manageable steps and then consistently executing those steps. Action is the bridge between wanting change and achieving it.

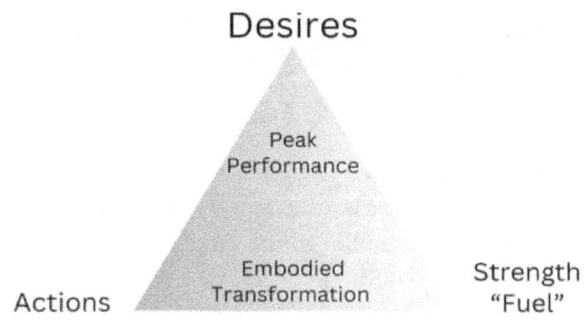

The key is that we must balance these three elements to make this framework effective. In other words, real change occurs when these three components are in harmony. It's like a three-legged stool—all parts need to be in balance for it to be stable and effective.

A balanced approach helps us adjust to changing circumstances. This way, we can tap into our embodied flow more naturally and sustainably. Our passion drives us, our actions are purposeful, and our strength keeps us going when things get tough.

On the flip side, too much desire without action causes frustration. Excessive action without strength risks injury. Strength without desire or action leads to stagnation.

Applying the Triangle of Change

1. **Constant evaluation:** Regularly check your triangle. Is your desire still blazing? Are your actions aligned with your ultimate goals? Is your strength at its peak?

2. **Adaptive mindset:** Be ready to shift focus between elements as conditions change. If progress stalls, focus on taking bold, calculated actions.

3. **Holistic development:** Use the triangle as a tool for comprehensive personal potential. As you grow in one area, it often positively impacts the others.

4. **Continuous progression:** The pursuit of excellence is never-ending and standing still means falling behind currency. Use the triangle of change as a framework for ongoing growth and adaptation.

5. **Synergy in the extreme:** Let each element amplify the others. The rush from a successful run (action) can skyrocket your desire, which in turn builds mind–body experiences filled with energy for learning potential.

Helicopter View Approach

Think of the helicopter approach like this: Imagine you're in a maze. When you're inside, all you see are the walls around you. But if you could fly up in a helicopter, you'd see the whole maze and easily spot the way out.

In the pursuit of peak potential, it's easy to get lost in the details. The helicopter approach allows us to rise above the immediate situation to observe it from a higher vantage point with a broader perspective.

This shift in perspective can reveal patterns, connections, and opportunities that may not be visible when you're immersed in the day-to-day grind. These insights are what separate great performers from good ones.

Moreover, the ability to see the big picture allows you to make decisions based on what's truly important, not just what's urgent. This enables you to maintain focus on long-term goals and better align your actions with mastery of embodied flow.

Implementing the helicopter approach involves regularly asking yourself key questions:

- *What is easy?*

- *What is difficult?*

- *Is there some other action I might "see" or try?*

- *Do I see something else to try differently or learn to put into the filing cabinet of observation?*

To effectively apply this approach, it's important to make it a regular practice. Set aside dedicated time for "helicopter up." This could be a few minutes of reflection before or after training sessions, or a weekly review of your progress and goals.

Replicating Success Patterns

Replicating patterns of success involves studying the strategies and techniques of high-achieving individuals and adapting those key elements to your own unique circumstances.

It's important to understand that replicating success patterns is not about simply mimicking what others have done. While you can certainly draw inspiration from the greats in your field, attempting to copy them exactly may not yield the same results. Instead, the goal is to identify the underlying principles that contribute to their success and then apply those principles in a way that aligns with your own strengths, weaknesses, and goals.

To develop a customizable framework for success, consider the following steps.

1. Identify Top Performers

Study individuals who consistently achieve high levels of success in your field. Analyze their background, experiences, and the challenges they've overcome to reach their current level of achievement.

2. Break Down Success Elements

Identify the core principles, strategies, and techniques that underlie their success. This requires cultivating accurate perceptive skill levels— the ability to discern patterns, connections, and essential factors that may not be immediately obvious. Carefully examine their actions, strategies, and outcomes, separating the truly crucial elements from the incidental ones. Verify your perceptions against objective data to ensure accuracy. The more precise and perceptive your analysis, the better you'll be able to distill the key drivers of their success. Determine which of these elements are most relevant and applicable to your own goals and circumstances, based on your keen understanding of their significance and context.

3. Create a Personalized Framework

Using the key elements you identified, develop a tailored success framework that aligns with your unique strengths and aspirations. Break down each element into specific, actionable strategies that you can implement in your daily life.

4. Practice and Refine

Apply your success framework in various contexts, both in training and real-world situations, until it becomes deeply ingrained in your mind–body–experience. This may take significant repetition—perhaps 40 times or more.

However, be mindful not to skip vital minute mini-steps in your progression. Many times, we may feel like we've stepped two steps forward, but if we've skipped essential foundational experiences, we may need to go back and retrain our mind–body from beginner flow experiences.

For example, in paragliding, a pilot might need to practice in light, fizzy thermals (with updrafts of 0.1 to 0.3 meters per second) and master these basics before progressing to stronger thermals (0.5 to 2 meters per second) in high winds, and all the variations in between. The turn radius and maintaining energy in the turn for the various conditions may require stepping backward to concentrate on training these skills before just concentrating on cross-country flights for distance. Time on the basic skills can be the possible answer to more efficiency in time for cross-country flights.

Continuously evaluate your progress and make adjustments based on your experiences and the feedback you receive. Be willing to revisit foundational skills and experiences as needed to ensure a solid base for further growth and development.

5. Seek Guidance and Support

Identify mentors or peers in your field who can provide guidance, feedback, and support as you work to replicate success patterns. Be open to their insights and suggestions, and be willing to adjust your approach based on their input. I've been working with coaches in Nordic skiing and paragliding for decades and found this invaluable in helping me move toward optimal peak performance when conditions align. Their guidance and support have been essential in refining my skills and making the most of my potential.

6. Embrace Continuous Learning

View the process of replicating success as an ongoing journey of growth and development rather than a one-time event. What worked yesterday may not work today, and what works today may not work tomorrow. Embrace challenges as opportunities for learning, and continuously seek out new knowledge and skills that can help you refine your framework over time.

The U.S. Women's National Soccer Team (USWNT) has consistently been one of the most successful teams in international soccer. They have won four World Cup titles (1991, 1999, 2015, and 2019) and four Olympic gold medals (1996, 2004, 2008, and 2012). A significant part of their success can be attributed to their ability to study and replicate the strategies and techniques of other successful teams.

Jill Ellis, who coached the USWNT from 2014 to 2019 and led them to two World Cup victories, has spoken about the team's approach to learning from others. In an interview with *Forbes*, Ellis mentioned that she and her staff would "watch a lot of games, analyze other teams, and try to replicate what they do well" (Leaders in Sport, 2020).

One specific example of this success pattern replication can be seen in the USWNT's development of their attacking style of play. In the years leading up to their 2015 and 2019 World Cup victories, the team studied the successful attacking strategies employed by top European clubs and national teams, such as Barcelona and the French national team.

By studying and incorporating these successful attacking patterns into their own game, the USWNT was able to develop a highly effective and entertaining style of play that helped them dominate on the international stage.

Recipe for Success Creation

Just as a master chef refines a recipe through careful experimentation and observation, you should identify and fine-tune the elements that contribute to your best performances. "To be successful, you have to create a recipe with the ingredients available to particular individuals," Theurillat explains (McClurg, 2021). "If you know this, success becomes something like a recipe. If you have several good ingredients and you mix them in the right way, you get a nice cake," he adds.

Identifying Your Success Ingredients

The "ingredients" in this performance recipe can vary widely depending on the individual and their sport. But they typically include **goal-setting**, **mind–body preparation**, **systematic approach** (detailed pre-performance checklists and consistent pre-performance routines), **environmental factors** (the readiness of your equipment, the appropriateness of the mother nature or playing field, and the level of support or competition from teammates or opponents), **work–life balance**, and **recovery.**

It's advisable to look beyond the obvious factors and consider subtle elements that might be easy to overlook. For instance, in his work with Chrigel Maurer, Theurillat helped identify seemingly minor factors that contributed significantly to Maurer's success. These included Maurer's tendency to perform his best when flying alone, without the distraction of other pilots. This insight led to strategic decisions, such as using a night pass early in a multiday event to help Maurer break away from the pack.

How to Set Effective Goals

Throughout this chapter, I've repeatedly mentioned and emphasized the importance of setting achievable goals. Learning to set goals is crucial because if you don't have a clear target in mind, how do you know what you're aiming for? It's like trying to shoot an arrow without a bull's-eye. You might get lucky and hit something, but chances are you'll just be flailing around aimlessly. Goals give you that tangible place for adaptation and evolving with flow.

But not all goals are gonna get you where you want to go. If you want to really crush it and find your flow, you need a solid mix of three different types of goals: performance, process, and mastery goals.

1. Performance Goals

Performance goals are your measurable targets. They're challenging yet achievable with effort. Think of a rock climber aiming to "send a 5.13a route within 6 months," or a big wave surfer setting out to "ride a 50-ft wave this season."

These goals give you direction and should be about your own standards. They're fundamentally different from ranking goals, which are often about winning the race, placing in the top, or outperforming others. I have to emphasize this distinction because ranking goals mostly involves external factors, which you can't control. Remember the circle of control approach we mentioned earlier? Ranking goals are variables that fall into the circle of concern, so they're essentially less useful here.

Meanwhile, performance goals create a more stable foundation for motivation and satisfaction. You gain skills, technique, and efficiency because you ensure that every single goal is within reach. You know you're thriving toward all achievable things as well as uncertainties.

2. Process Goals

While performance goals define the destination, process goals chart the course. These are the day-to-day actions and behaviors that pave the way to your desired outcomes. Process goals are all about the "how"— the specific actions you'll take to reach your performance goals. They encompass your daily habits, training routines, and mind–body preparation.

For our rock climber aiming for that 5.13a route, process goals might include

- "Complete hang-board workouts 3 times a week, focusing on finger strength"

- "Practice visualization of the route for 15 minutes before each climbing session"

- "Analyze and refine technique on similar routes twice a week"

- "Maintain a balanced diet with adequate protein intake for muscle recovery"

- "Engage in 20 minutes of mindfulness meditation daily to enhance focus"

As you create your process goals, make them as specific as possible. Vague goals like "practice more" or "eat healthier" are difficult to measure and stick to. Instead, define the exact actions you will take, the frequency, and the duration.

You also need to ensure that these process goals directly support and enable your performance goals. Each process goal should move you closer to your peak performance vision.

3. Mastery Goals

The "how" is everything you need for success, and mastery goals help to ensure this. They're all about PERFECTING by getting into the nitty-gritty of the techniques, strategies, and mind–body games that let you perform at your best. A real master doesn't just follow a plan; they know the "how" inside and out. That's why they can tweak their approach on the fly to handle whatever comes their way.

As peak performance expert Theurillat explains, while working on mastering something, the process teaches you how to do the "how" right. He notes,

> If you look at the ancient martial arts, they only focus on the mastery goal because they have over a thousand years of experience. If they are a master, they will handle the how. If they handle how they win the fight. (McClurg, 2021, p. 205)

So, what goes into creating mastery goals? First off, you've gotta be deeply curious and ready to geek out on every little detail of what you're doing. It means breaking things down to the basics, analyzing each part, and putting it all back together in a way that clicks for you. It's about practicing, getting feedback, and fine-tuning your mind–body over and over.

Creating a Recipe of Success

Once these "ingredients" are identified, the next step is to create a repeatable process for combining them effectively. This might involve

1. **Developing pre-performance routines that consistently put you in the optimal mind–body:**

   o Create a detailed timeline for the hours leading up to performance.

   o Include physical warm-up exercises specific to your sport.

   o Incorporate mind–body preparation techniques.

   o Establish a nutrition and hydration plan.

   o Set up environment checks (e.g., equipment preparation and the intricate variables of mother nature familiarization).

2. **Creating decision-making frameworks for use during performance:**

   o Develop a set of "if-then" scenarios for common situations.

   o Create a mind–body checklist for rapid assessment of changing conditions.

   o Establish clear criteria for go/no-go decisions.

   o Practice quick decision-making drills to improve in-the-moment choices.

3. **Establishing post-performance review and recovery processes:**

   o Design a structured cool-down routine.

- Create a template for performance analysis and reflection.

- Set up a system for gathering feedback from coaches or teammates.

- Plan recovery activities (e.g., nutrition, sleep, and active recovery).

- Schedule time for mind–body reset and preparation for the next challenge.

This "recipe" isn't meant to be rigid. As Theurillat noted in our earlier discussion, different individuals might find success under different conditions.

A paraglider might find that their recipe includes studying weather patterns for 30 minutes each morning, including analyzing skew T diagrams. Skew T diagrams are charts used in meteorology to predict atmospheric conditions, which can help paragliders plan their route for the day and decide what to wear based on the expected conditions at cloud base (the bottom of the cloud layer). This weather analysis might then be followed by 15 minutes of visualization. A business executive, on the other hand, might discover that their peak performance comes after a 5 a.m. workout and 20 minutes of meditation. The key is to identify these personal success factors and learn to recreate them consistently.

Even the most well-crafted recipe must allow for flexibility and adaptability. In the dynamic world of sports, particularly in outdoor sports like paragliding, conditions can change rapidly. A sudden shift in wind patterns or shading, for example, might require a paraglider to quickly adjust their strategy mid-flight. Similarly, a business executive might need to adapt their approach in response to a sudden market shift or unexpected challenge. Therefore, a truly effective performance recipe must include not only the core ingredients for success but also strategies for adapting to all the what-ifs or unexpected situations.

Personalizing Your Flow Practice

In the course of this chapter, we've explored a range of strategies and frameworks designed to help you create your own embodied-flow practice for peak performance. From setting goals to developing contingency plans, from leveraging the power of the circle of control to mastering the art of incremental growth through the triangle of change, we've covered extensive ground and filled our toolbox ready for unleashing peak performance potential.

But there's one crucial piece we haven't yet discussed—a piece that, in many ways, is the keystone that holds the entire arch of our practice together.

Understanding your personal flow landscape is similar to charting a topographic map of your embodied flow experiences—identifying the peaks of intense engagement and the valleys of distraction. This awareness is essential because no matter how well-designed our strategies are or how solid our frameworks may be, their effectiveness depends on our ability to apply them to our current circumstances.

To gain this critical understanding, we can employ a simple yet practical assessment technique inspired by Theurillat's question-based coaching approach: "On a scale from 1 to 10, with 10 representing you having all the skills and the mindset and you're totally present, and 1 being the opposite, where are you at right now, today?" (McClurg, 2021, p. 203).

This question prompts you to check in with yourself and create a snapshot of your current perspective. However, its true power lies in the follow-up reflections it elicits:

If you find yourself at a 6, the natural next questions are: Why a 6? What specific factors contribute to that score? Perhaps you're feeling particularly focused and in flow with your physical training, but you're struggling with mind–body blocks related to competition unknowns. This realization can lead to targeted interventions, such as incorporating more visualization exercises or mind–body rehearsal techniques to address those competition-related challenges.

Conversely, if you rate yourself a 9, riding high on a recent breakthrough, the key questions become: What's working so well? How can you codify and replicate these conditions? This high score presents an opportunity to analyze and document the factors contributing to your success. Are you following a particular routine? Have you made changes to your training regimen? Understanding these elements can help you maintain this high level of performance and potentially push it even further.

How about a lower score, such as a 3? It's definitely fine. In fact, it's a valuable data point. The questions here might be: What's your struggle? What small step could you take to move from a 3 to a 3.1? Making a dramatic leap from a 3 to a 10 shortly is highly unlikely and can be counterproductive. Putting that kind of pressure on yourself can lead to frustration and disappointment, which can hinder your progress. Instead, focusing on small, achievable improvements can set you on a sustainable upward trajectory. This approach aligns with the concept of a positive spiral discussed earlier.

As Theurillat shares,

> It's totally okay wherever you are on the scale. Sometimes, we have clients, and we ask them: "Where are you between 1 and 10?" And they tell me they are minus one hundred. That's totally okay. Then we try to get to minus 99. If everyone is between 1 and 10, we force you to think about where you are and how we can stabilize it if you are high, or how we can improve it if you are low. (McClurg, 2021, p. 203)

As we conclude this chapter, I invite you to make the 1–10 question a regular part of your embodied-flow practice. Set aside time each day, if possible, or at least each week or month, to check in with yourself during your practice sessions. Ask the question, reflect on your answers, and use those insights to inform your next steps. With each reflection and each action, you're not just practicing embodied flow—you're embodying it, making it a part of who you are and how you move through the world toward your peak performance potential.

Conclusion

As I sit here, penning these final thoughts, I'm struck by the paradox of concluding a book about something as boundless as flow. It feels akin to trying to bottle a river—the moment you think you've grasped it, it slips through your fingers, rushing onward to new horizons.

This exploration has taken us from the neuroscience labs to the peaks of mountains, from the focused silence of meditation cushions to the heart-pounding exhilaration of extreme sports. We've uncovered a truth both simple and profound: Flow isn't just an experience we stumble into, but a skill we can cultivate, a practice we can embody. It's a gateway to unlocking our full potential and achieving peak performance in all areas of life.

The numbers speak volumes: a 500% boost in productivity, a 430% surge in creativity, and athletes performing at levels 2–3 times above their average (McKinsey & Company, n.d.; Kotler, 2014; Flow Genome Project, 2016). Yet, beyond these impressive statistics lies something even more compelling—the quiet revolution happening in lives across the globe as more people tap into the transformative influence or potential of flow.

Flow challenges our conventional notions of being and reality. Time warps and consciousness merges with action, hinting at mind–body–environment capacities far beyond everyday perceptions. If these experiences are accessible through practice and training, what else might be possible? What other aspects of human potential remain untapped or untappable simply because we haven't figured out how to access them yet?

Your journey into flow is uniquely yours. It begins with honest reflection. What lights you up? Where do you lose track of time? These are your clues, the breadcrumbs leading you toward your embodied-flow mindset and peak performance potential for sport, business, work, and life. As you embark on this path, remember that rewiring your brain isn't an overnight process. It takes 21–66 days of consistent practice to forge new neural pathways (Science of Mind, 2024). Choose your focus wisely, considering what changes you're willing to commit to, day in and day out. Start small, but start today.

Clear intentions, structured plans, and daily practices of mindfulness, breath work, and movement form the cornerstones of your flow practice. Yet equally important is the recognition of rest and recovery—it's in these quiet moments that integration happens, preparing you for the next challenge. This balance of effort and ease mirrors the winding road of embodied flow mastery, full of unexpected turns and breathtaking vistas. Embrace every twist in the journey, for each setback is a setup for a breakthrough.

We stand on the cusp of movement toward mastering a flow revolution. Wearable tech and virtual reality are opening new frontiers in training and performance optimization. The principles of embodied flow are seeping into boardrooms and classrooms, hospitals, and homes. Even the military is exploring embodied-flow mindsets to enhance performance under pressure. As this awareness spreads, we can expect to see flow practices woven into the fabric of daily life.

Schools may be redesigned to foster intrinsic motivation for learning, encouraging students to find joy and engagement in the process of discovery itself. Workplaces might be restructured around principles of deep work and peak experiences, allowing employees and entrepreneurs alike to tap into states of heightened creativity and productivity. This shift toward integrating flow into our daily environments has the potential to transform how we approach education, work, and personal development.

Of course, this journey demands a willingness to face perceptual reality, to embrace setbacks as a faithful mentor, and to surrender cherished ideas of who we are in the fires of transformation. There will be times of doubt, of disorientation, of taking a different path off our main journey in the thickets of our own becoming. This is all part of the sacred process, the shedding of skins that is the definitive decisive action for a life of authentic embodiment and peak performance.

So, where do you go from here? Begin by setting clear intentions and creating a daily routine that incorporates elements of embodied flow, no matter how small. Seek out challenges that push you just beyond your current abilities and surround yourself with others on this path—their energy will fuel your own. Stay curious and open, for the moment you think you've mastered flow is the moment you begin to lose it. This is a lifelong practice, an endless exploration of what's possible when we align mind, body, and world in purposeful action.

Looking ahead to my ongoing journey with flow, I'm filled with anticipation for the adventures to come. My future aspirations include mastering the art of carving—whether it's riding thermals in a paraglider, gliding effortlessly on cross-country skis, or pursuing the efficient arced edge-to-edge turns on alpine slopes. Each discipline offers its own lessons in efficiency, smoothness, and harmony with the natural world, and I'm excited to discover how these experiences will further illuminate aspects of everyday life and push the boundaries of human potential.

As we close this chapter, know that the real adventure is just beginning. The blueprint for embodying flow is in your hands now. Use it. Refine it. Make it your own. Remember, you're part of a growing community of passionate individuals committed to pushing the boundaries of human potential.

Embrace the challenges that lie ahead. Let uncertainty be your guide, not your adversary. Make it work for you instead of against you. Every time you step into the unknown, you're giving yourself a chance to evolve in ways you've yet to conceive. It's apparent that even the most accomplished individuals were once novices. What sets them apart? Their unwavering commitment to push forward, to lean into the discomfort, to dance with uncertainty. I'm calling you to join this dance—are you ready to discover the extraordinary within you?

And along the way, don't forget to celebrate the victories to come, but hold them lightly. And never, ever stop exploring the limitless possibilities of your own embodied experience. When we live authentically and share our talents, we inspire others to do the same. We become examples for others, showing what's possible when we push our limits. Each of us contributes something unique to the world, helping create a society that's more creative and full of potential.

The thermals are rising. The mountains are calling. The canvas of your potential stretches out before you, vast and inviting. What masterpiece will you create? Let us meet this great adventure of embodied flow with wonder, with curiosity, with hearts wide open to the mystery. Let us have the courage to continually choose the paths that awaken and enliven us, trusting that they will lead us ever more deeply into the heartland of our own native genius.

Your journey continues. So does mine. I hope our paths cross out there, in the arena of life where theory meets practice and the real magic happens. I look forward to hearing about your flow experiences and the unique twists and turns of your journey. Now, take a deep breath. Feel the potential coursing through you. And take that next step into mastering embodied flow potential.

About the Author

Johnna Haskell is a passionate adventurer and educator, constantly seeking transformative experiences in sports, flying, and everyday life.

With a PhD in education focusing on flow pedagogy and outdoor embodied experience, Johnna brings a unique blend of academic rigor and practical adventure to her work. Her diverse background includes freelance wildlife photography, science education, administration, and over 18 years of university teaching before returning to her true passion: sharing insights into the mind–body world.

Johnna's outdoor pursuits span a wide range of activities, including canoeing, kayaking, skiing, rock and ice climbing, backpacking, mountaineering, and paragliding. Her notable achievements include summiting Denali (20,320 ft) and attempting to paraglide off the peak of Kilimanjaro (19,341 ft) as part of a major charity event supporting water supplies in various African communities.

When not exploring the globe with her paraglider or scaling mountains, Johnna dedicates her time to teaching Nordic cross-country ski instructors, sharing her passion for both classic and skate skiing techniques. She also pursues her interest in aviation by learning to fly motorgliders.

Johnna has committed her life to helping athletes and individuals harness their mental strength to achieve their full potential. Her research and strategies have inspired coaches, athletes, and instructors across all levels to strive for and attain their personal best.

Her academic credentials include a PhD in curriculum studies/science education, with extensive research in flow pedagogy of outdoor education. She also holds an MSEd in educational leadership and a BS in animal science, complemented by minors in studio art and outdoor education. This multidisciplinary background enables Johnna to approach peak performance and flow states from a holistic, well-rounded perspective.

Did you enjoy reading *Mastering Embodied Flow Mindset*?

Thank you for dedicating your time to exploring this book. I sincerely hope you found the journey both enlightening and rewarding.

If you discovered value in *Mastering Embodied Flow Mindset: Unleashing Peak Performance Potential in Sports and Life*, would you consider sharing your thoughts in a brief Amazon review? Your perspective, even just a sentence or two, could be instrumental in helping others discover this resource and embark on their own journey of personal growth.

Your review could help reach more readers!

As I continue to write and explore these concepts further, I invite you to stay connected. For updates on new releases, exclusive content, and special offers, please join our community at epicleafinnovations.com

Join our community at EpicLeafInnovations.com

I'm always eager to hear about your experiences, insights, or questions. Please don't hesitate to reach out at info@epicleafinnovations.com. Your feedback and stories are invaluable in shaping future work and fostering a community of like-minded individuals.

Wishing you continued success in your pursuit of flow and peak performance,

Johnna Haskell

References

The Adrenaline Zone. (n.d.). *Born survivor and wingsuit flyer Jeb Corliss.* https://www.theadrenalinezone.com/episodes/jeb-corliss-wingsuit-base-jumper

Akiskalian, E. (2004, May 17). *Shane Dorian interview from the 2004 Towsurfer vault.* Towsurfer. https://towsurfer.com/2017/05/shane-dorian-interview-from-the-2004-towsurfer-vault/

Baumgartner, G. (2020, April 2). *Michael Strasser: How he beats his mental challenges.* Red Bull. https://www.redbull.com/int-en/michael-strasser-extreme-athlete-mindset-interview

Bompa, T. O., & Haff, G. G. (2009). *Periodization: Theory and methodology of training.* Human Kinetics.

Boukreev, A. (2001). *Above the clouds: The diaries of a high-altitude mountaineer* (L. Wylie, Ed.). St. Martin's Press.

Brisius, A. (2022). *Chasing the white whale: My struggle with flow addiction.* Mindful Press.

Bubbs, M. (2019). *Peak: The new science of athletic performance that is revolutionizing sports.* Chelsea Green Publishing.

Burke, L. M., Hawley, J. A., Wong, S. H. S., & Jeukendrup, A. E. (2011). Carbohydrates for training and competition. *Journal of Sports Sciences, 29*(S1), S17-S27. https://doi.org/10.1080/02640414.2011.585473

Brisick, J. (2024, March 26). Shane Dorian. *The Surfer's Journal, Soundings, 5*(11). https://www.surfersjournal.com/editorial/soundings-shane-dorian/

Brown, M. (2023). *How did Courtney Dauwalter get so damn fast?* Outside Online. https://www.outsideonline.com/outdoor-adventure/courtney-dauwalter/

Caldwell, T. (2017). *The push: A climber's journey of endurance, risk, and going beyond limits.* Penguin.

Colombetti, G. (2014). *The feeling body: Affective science meets the enactive mind.* MIT Press.

Cook, G. (2010). *Movement: Functional movement systems: Screening, assessment, corrective strategies.* On Target Publications.

Covey, S. R. (1989). *The 7 habits of highly effective people: Powerful lessons in personal change.* Free Press.

Craig, A. D. (2009). How do you feel—now? The anterior insula and human awareness. *Nature Reviews Neuroscience, 10*(1), 59–70. https://doi.org/10.1038/nrn2555

Cross Country Magazine. (2020, April 17). *Cross Country interviews: Chrigel Maurer* [Video]. YouTube. https://www.youtube.com/watch?v=IVSeBZQmdGk

Cross Country Magazine. (2021a, February 5). *Always listen to the feeling.* https://xcmag.com/fly-better/paragliding-techniques-paramotoring-skills/always-listen-to-the-feeling/

Cross Country Magazine. (2021b, June 6). *Chrigel Maurer and Thomas Theurillat finish at the top.* https://www.xcmag.com/2021/06/chrigel-maurer-and-thomas-theurillat-finish-at-the-top

Cross Country Magazine. (2023a, March 15). *Red Bull X-Alps: Chrigel Maurer's planning strategies.* https://xcmag.com/news/red-bull-x-alps-2023-watch-chrigel-maurers-reaction-to-the-route/

Cross Country Magazine. (2023b, June 6). *Red Bull X-Alps 2023: Chrigel switches out supporters.* Cross Country Magazine. https://xcmag.com/news/red-bull-x-alps-2023-chrigel-switches-out-supporters/

Crum, A. J. (2020). Rethinking stress: The role of mindsets in determining the stress response. *Journal of Personality and Social Psychology,* *118*(6), 1031–1046. https://doi.org/10.1037/pspp0000207

Csikszentmihalyi, M. (1975). *Beyond boredom and anxiety: Experiencing flow in work and play.* Jossey-Bass.

Csikszentmihalyi, M. (1990). *Flow: The psychology of optimal experience.* Harper & Row.

Cuddy, A. (2015). *Presence: Bringing your boldest self to your biggest challenges.* Little, Brown Spark.

Damasio, A. R. (1994). *Descartes' error: Emotion, reason, and the human brain.* Putnam.

de Manzano, Ö., Cervenka, S., Jucaite, A., Hellenäs, O., Farde, L., & Ullén, F. (2013). Individual differences in the proneness to have flow experiences are linked to dopamine D2-receptor availability in the dorsal striatum. *NeuroImage, 67,* 1–6. https://doi.org/10.1016/j.neuroimage.2012.10.072

Dietrich, A., & McDaniel, W. F. (2004). Endocannabinoids and exercise. *British Journal of Sports Medicine, 38*(5), 536–541.

Diggins, J. (2020, July 22). *Training fuel, part 2: The actual food.* Jessie Diggins. https://jessiediggins.com/training-fuel-part-2-the-actual-food/

Diggins, J., & Smith, T. (2020). *Brave enough.* University of Minnesota Press.

Dimmler, J. (2020). *Cross-country tips by Chrigel Maurer.* The Paraglider. https://www.theparaglider.com/cross-country-tips-by-chrigel-maurer

Dougall, S. (2023, June 20). *Flow at work: Unleash your professional potential and find fulfillment.* LinkedIn. https://www.linkedin.com/pulse/flow-work-unleash-your-professional-potential-find-shannon-dougall/

Dreyfus, H. L. (2005). Overcoming the myth of the mental: How philosophers can profit from the phenomenology of everyday expertise. *Proceedings and Addresses of the American Philosophical Association, 79*(2), 47–65. https://doi.org/10.2307/30046278

Express Staff. (2016, May 25). *Ketchum woman summits Mount Everest for 6th time: Melissa Arnot is first U.S. woman to summit without supplemental oxygen.* Idaho Mountain Express. https://www.mtexpress.com/news/blaine_county/ketchum-woman-summits-mount-everest-for-th-time/article_4c4e15a0-2200-11e6-aaaa-97a0eb92ff9b.html

Farina, K. (2019). *Mastering paragliding.* Cross Country International Ltd.

Feldenkrais, M. (1972). *Awareness through movement: Health exercises for personal growth.* Harper & Row.

Flow Genome Project. (n.d.). *Flow performance: Harness the power of peak states.* https://www.flowgenomeproject.com/flow-performance

Gervais, M. (2020). *Mastering fear: Human potential.* Macmillan.

Graepel, S. (2017, June 27). *Kilian Jornet: The Everest interview.* GearJunkie. https://gearjunkie.com/endurance/kilian-jornet-mount-everest-interview

Gucciardi, D. F., Gordon, S., & Dimmock, J. A. (2010). Advancing mental toughness research and theory using personal construct psychology. *International Review of Sport and Exercise Psychology, 2*(1), 54–72.

Gupta, S. S. (2024). *The challenge of climbing Everest without oxygen! | Conrad Anker* [Video]. YouTube. https://www.youtube.com/watch?v=eno7AisHvy0

Henri, R. (1923). *The art spirit.* Lippincott.

Hof, W. (2020). *The Wim Hof method: Activate your full human potential.* Sounds True.

Hoolihan, C. (2022, June 13). *Using heart rate variability to maximize performance.* IDEA. https://www.ideafit.com/personal-training/using-heart-rate-variability-to-maximize-performance/

Honnold, A., & Roberts, D. (2015). *Alone on the wall.* W. W. Norton & Company.

International Olympic Committee. (n.d.). *Jessie Diggins: It's all about teamwork* [Video]. https://olympics.com/en/video/jessie-diggins-its-all-about-teamwork

ISPO. (n.d.). *Courtney Dauwalter.* https://www.ispo.com/en/heroes/courtney-dauwalter

Jackson, P., & Delehanty, H. (2013). *Eleven rings: The soul of success.* Penguin Books.

Janda, V. (1983). *Muscle function testing.* Butterworths.

Jarvis, C. (2017, October 27). *Shane Dorian interview: Bring in priority for Big Wave events.* Towsurfer. https://towsurfer.com/2017/10/shane-dorian-interview-bring-in-priority-for-big-wave-events/

Talk North Podcast Network. (2020, April 6). *Jessie Diggins: "Don't be afraid of the Pain Cave".*

https://talknorth.com/2020/04/06/jessie-diggins-dont-be-afraid-of-the-pain-cave/

JRE Podcast. (2023, October 26). *Joe Rogan Experience #2052 - Shane Dorian.* https://www.jrepodcast.com/episode/joe-rogan-experience-2052-shane-dorian

Karageorghis, C. I. (2017). *Applying music in exercise and sport.* Human Kinetics.

Kotler, S. (2014). *The rise of Superman: Decoding the science of ultimate human performance.* New Harvest.

Kotler, S. (2022, August 31). *Flow trigger: The challenge/skill ratio.* Flow Research Collective. https://www.flowresearchcollective.com/blog/flow-trigger-the-challenge-skill-ratio

Leaders in Sport. (2020, November 19). *Leaders Performance Podcast: At home with Leaders - Jill Ellis* [Audio podcast]. Leaders Performance Institute. https://leadersinsport.com/performance-institute/podcasts/podcast-at-home-with-leaders-jill-ellis/

Mast, F. (2024, April 14). *Olympic skier Jessie Diggins in workout gear goes on hiking honeymoon in Chile.* CelebWell. https://celebwell.com/olympic-skier-jessie-diggins-goes-on-hiking-honeymoon-in-chile/

Maurer, C. (2016). 'Analysis and self-reflection' with Chrigel Maurer [Interview]. *Cross Country Magazine.* https://xcmag.com/magazine-articles/analysis-and-self-reflection-with-chrigel-maurer/

McClurg, G. (2020, May 22). Episode 119- Yael Margelisch and building confidence. *Cloudbase Mayhem.*

https://www.cloudbasemayhem.com/episode-119-yael-margelisch-and-building-confidence/

McClurg, G. (2021). *Advanced paragliding: What I've learned from the world's best pilots.* Cross Country International.

McGill, S. (2015). *Back mechanic: The step-by-step McGill Method to fix back pain.* Backfitpro Incorporated.

McKinsey & Company. (n.d.). *The role of flow in improving productivity.* https://www.mckinsey.com/capabilities/people-and-organizational-performance/our-insights/increasing-the-meaning-quotient-of-work

Merleau-Ponty, M. (1964). *The primacy of perception: And other essays on phenomenological psychology, the philosophy of art, history and politics* (J. M. Edie, Ed.). Northwestern University Press.

Miller, C. C. (2021, March 26). Why some athletes seemingly can't stop chasing their high. *The New York Times.* https://www.nytimes.com/2021/03/26/health/flow-state-addiction.html

Miller, E. (2013, April 11). Rock climber, base jumper Steph Davis: Flying fearless. *Boulder Weekly.* https://archives.boulderweekly.com/adventure/rock-climber-base-jumper-steph-davis-flying-fearless/

Nakamura, J., & Csikszentmihalyi, M. (2002). The concept of flow. In C. R. Snyder & S. J. Lopez (Eds.), *Handbook of Positive Psychology* (pp. 89–105). Oxford University Press. https://doi.org/10.1093/oxfordhb/9780195187243.001.0001

P3 - Peak Performance Project. (2021). *Our story.* https://p3.md/our-story/

Porges, S. W. (2011). *The polyvagal theory: Neurophysiological foundations of emotions, attachment, communication, and self-regulation.* W. W. Norton & Company.

Red Bull X-Alps. (2021, June 28). *Chrigel did it again!* https://www.redbullxalps.com/int-en/chrigel-did-it-again

Restak, R. (2009). *Think smart: A neuroscientist's prescription for improving your brain's performance.* Riverhead Books.

Sawka, M. N., Burke, L. M., Eichner, E. R., Maughan, R. J., Montain, S. J., & Stachenfeld, N. S. (2007). Exercise and fluid replacement. *Medicine and Science in Sports and Exercise, 39*(2), 377–390. https://doi.org/10.1249/mss.0b013e31802ca597

Schmidt, R. A. (2003). Motor schema theory after 27 years: Reflections and implications for a new theory. *Research Quarterly for Exercise and Sport, 74*(4), 366–375. https://doi.org/10.1080/02701367.2003.10609106

Seligman, M. E. P. (2011). *Flourish: A visionary new understanding of happiness and well-being.* Free Press.

Shah, V. (2017, October 20). *A conversation with Jeb Corliss, wingsuit pilot, BASE jumper & shark diver.* Thought Economics. https://thoughteconomics.com/jeb-corliss/

Sheets-Johnstone, M. (2011). *The primacy of movement* (2nd ed.). John Benjamins Publishing Company.

Shiffrin, M. (2019). *Rise: My story.* Harper.

Siegel, R. D. (2010). *The mindfulness solution: Everyday practices for everyday problems.* Guilford Press.

Sims, S. (2016). *ROAR: How to match your food and fitness to your unique female physiology for optimum performance, great health, and a strong, lean body for life.* Rodale Books.

Starrett, K. (2013). *Becoming a supple leopard: The ultimate guide to resolving pain, preventing injury, and optimizing athletic performance.* Victory Belt Publishing.

Stulberg, B., & Magness, S. (2017). *Peak performance: Elevate your game, avoid burnout, and thrive with the new science of success.* Rodale Books.

Suzuki, W. (2023, September 13). *Effects of exercise on your brain.* Dana Foundation. https://dana.org/resources/effects-of-exercise-on-your-brain-with-wendy-suzuki/

Shinn, P. (2021, December 2). *Jessie Diggins—The defending Olympic champion—talks about her priorities this season.* Team USA. https://www.teamusa.com/news/2021/december/02/jessie-diggins-talks-about-her-priorities-this-season

Theyerl, B. (2024, January 23). *Home team energy—Head coach, Matt Whitcomb.* FasterSkier. https://fasterskier.com/2024/01/home-team-energy-head-coach-matt-whitcomb/

Thomas, T., Erdman, K. A., & Burke, L. M. (2016). Position of the Academy of Nutrition and Dietetics, Dietitians of Canada, and the American College of Sports Medicine: Nutrition and athletic performance. *Journal of the Academy of Nutrition and Dietetics, 116*(3), 501–528. https://doi.org/10.1016/j.jand.2015.12.006

Roychowdhury, D. (2023, June 7). *Using mental rehearsal to boost your performance and well-being in sport and exercise.* https://www.drdevroy.com/mental-rehearsal-in-sport-and-exercise/

U.S. Ski & Snowboard. (n.d.). *Jessie Diggins.* https://usskiandsnowboard.org/athletes/jessie-diggins

Viesturs, E., & Roberts, D. (2006). *No shortcuts to the top: Climbing the world's 14 highest peaks.* Broadway Books.

Viesturs, E., & Roberts, D. (2011). *The will to climb: Obsession and commitment and the quest to climb Annapurna--the world's deadliest peak.* Crown Publishing Group.

Vranich, B. (2020). *Breathe: The simple, revolutionary 14-day program to improve your mental and physical health.* St. Martin's Essentials.

Weil, A. (2016). *Breathing: The master key to self healing.* Sounds True.

Wotruba, D., Michels, L., Buechler, R., Metzler, S., Theodoridou, A., Gerstenberg, M., Walitza, S., Kollias, S., Rössler, W., & Heekeren, K. (2014). Aberrant coupling within and across the default mode, task-positive, and salience network in subjects at risk for psychosis. *Schizophrenia Bulletin, 40*(5), 1095–1104. https://doi.org/10.1093/schbul/sbt161

Wulf, G. (2013). Attentional focus and motor learning: A review of 15 years. *International Review of Sport and Exercise Psychology, 6*(1), 77–104. https://doi.org/10.1080/1750984X.2012.723728